REARRANGED, NEVER THE SAME: THE NATURE OF GRIEF

BY

DEVA JOY GOUSS, LCSW

For Momsy and Mymi
In honor of
Love's Eternal Nature

TABLE OF CONTENTS

Introduction
The Intention and Overview of This Book
The Inevitable Membership into the Club

THE NATURE OF GRIEF
1 "It Just Sucks"..1
2 Re-arranged, Never the Same...2
3 There is Nothing Linear About Grieving.........................4
4 Grieving is an Individual Experience.................................5
5 The Front Burner, Back Burner Phenomenon................6
6 Riding the Waves 7
7 Impermanence is an Absolute..9

SURRENDERING...11
8 Surrendering into Grief..12
9 "Gone"..13
10 Longing is Your New Companion..................................15
11 The Doorway into Vulnerability 16
12 When Death is Unexpected..18
13 When Suicide Happens..20
14 Every Loss Brings Us Closer To Our Own Mortality ..23

THE MENTAL GYMNASTICS OF THE GRIEVING MIND ..25
15 "If Only... If Only... What If..." 26
16 "I Just Want Her Back..."...28
17 Remorse..29
18 Obsessing about the Last Moments...............................30
19 Unfinished Business..32
20 One Loss Brings Up All Loss...33
21 The Grief Channel 34
22 How Mortality Impacts Loving 35

HOW TO NAVIGATE THROUGH GRIEF 39
23 Making it Through a Day 40
24 Give Permission to All of Your Feelings 41
25 Let Others Know You Are "Grieving".........................43
26 You Can't Tell Grief to Go Away But You Can Learn to
    "Bracket" It 45
27 Ways to Spend Time With the Grief 46
28 Meditation Practice...48
29 The Power of Mantra...51
30 Intentionally Change the Grief Channel 53

31 Differentiate between Healthy and Unhealthy Grief.................54

32 Seeking Professional Help.................56

33 When You First Met Death.................57

34 Keep Breathing and Keep Holding Hands.................59

35 The Forgiveness Process.................60

36 The Challenges to Receiving Support.................63

37 The Power of Words.................65

38 Honoring the Heart's Wisdom.................67

39 For Those Supporting the Bereaved 68

THE SILVER LINING.................71

40 Is There A Silver Lining, Please? 72

41 Whole Includes the Hole.................73

42 Moving Towards Being Present.................74

43 Is it Okay For Me to Enjoy My Life Again?.................77

44 The Unity in Grief.................79

45 "Back To Life".................81

TWO HANDS – One Hand; Grief, One Hand; Connection 83

46 Two Hands.................84

47 Staying in Current Relationship 86

48 Ways of Opening to Connection.................88

49 "No Birth, No Death".................89

50 Pop The Balloon.................91

51 Waves of the Ocean.................92

COMMUNICATIONS FROM MOM.................93

52 Conversations with Momsy.................94

53 Mom Visits Me.................96

54 Mom Sends Me a Letter.................97

55 Mom Surprises Me at the Pool.................98

56 Mom Comforts Me.................100

57 Mom Comments on My "Things to Do" List.................101

58 Mom Shares Important Information.................102

59 Mom Guides Me Away From Grief 103

60 Mom Enlightens Me.................105

61 Mom's Letter To A Women's Gathering.................106

EXPERIENCES OF GRIEF FROM FELLOW CLUB MEMBERS...111

Britt.................112

Lisa.................115

Janie.................116

Jeffree.................118

Ellen..121

Shaun...123

Renee...127

Devajoy..129

62 Nothing Diminishes Love..144

63 The Chapter that Follows After The Book Is Written..............145

The presence of that absence is everywhere.
— Edna St. Vincent Millay

INTRODUCTION

Loss of a loved one is like an earthquake that ravages the ground beneath us. It changes the landscape of everything we know and of life as we lived it. Even the sturdiest, most stable structures can crumble during a quake. And often, so do our lives.

Earthquakes change landscapes forever.

Rearranged, never the same.

Grief is like nothing else. It brings us to our knees as we reckon with the fact that there is nothing we can do to bring back our loved one and the lives we once knew.

In the devastation of the quake, it feels like the heart breaks over and over again into a trillion pieces, transforming our lives in ways that we could not have imagined or desired.

Earthquakes can change the landscape but the land itself does not cease to exist — and nor do we. Our lives continue, although severely jagged. The fact that we go on living is often an amazing feat in and of itself.

A mysterious strength from within reveals itself and takes us through. Just like Mother Earth, we keep on going.

THE INTENTION AND
OVERVIEW OF THIS BOOK

Grief is such a tender and raw time. I have no fantasies that this book will take away your pain in any way or even soften the blow of the unfathomable harsh reality of impermanence.

I have no illusion that I can lessen your sense of loss. I wish I could.

I wish I had a magic wand to make it different than it is. I wish I could make it easier for you. I wish I could offer you some shortcut – or something - that would ease the pain.

But with grief, there are no shortcuts, no magic bullets, and there is no fixing it.

I encourage you to know that you have to go through your own grieving process in your own way and that no one can tell you how that should be. No one can change how it feels for you, make it stop hurting, or tell you how to live your grieving process.

From my own experience of grief and as a psychotherapist, I have found that there is a vast common ground of shared experiences that occurs with loss and grieving — similar thought patterns, feelings, regrets, symptoms of distress, and reactions to the trauma of loss. I refer to this common ground as "the nature of grief." Whether one is grieving a spouse, a brother, a mother, a child, a friend, a lover, an animal companion, there is a shared experience in grief that reveals that we are not alone, even when we feel very alone. Understanding the nature of grief can help us to surrender to the experience and allow it to be what it is; it gives permission to experience whatever arises and to accept that there is a normalcy to our feelings and thoughts in such an abnormal time.

This book covers everything I have learned about the nature of grief. In the first two sections, "The Nature of Grief" and "Surrendering," I document every theme I have witnessed in the grieving process, through my own experiences and by observing and sitting with the grief of my friends, family, and psychotherapy clients. In the third section, "The Mental Gymnastics of the Grieving Mind," repetitive thought patterns that arise in the grief process are described and examined. In the fourth section, "How to Navigate Through Grief," I explore ways of making it through the day, including how to decipher between healthy and unhealthy grieving, asking for help, meditation tools, journaling, ritual, and other exercises. The fifth section, "The Silver Lining," focuses on the integrating of grief into your being so that in time, you grow to enjoy your life again.

In section six, "Two Hands - One Hand Grief; One Hand, Connection," the focus of the book shifts from loss to the ongoing connection with your loved one. It explores how to be open to the prospect of staying in contact – or as I call it "current relationship" – with the one who has departed. In section seven, called "Communications from Mom," I share the relevant communications I received from my mother after she left her body. It is my experience that she came to me at least ten times in which she shared significant guidance that I now want to share with others.

In the last section, "Experiences of Grief from Fellow Club Members," several people share their experiences with grief. I also include excerpts from my memoir called *Stripped to the Core* that I wrote soon after my mother transitioned. These pages describe the experience of sitting vigil during the descent of my mother's life and the profound release that accompanied her transition. My hope is that people will relate to the shared stories and allow for the company of others in the bereavement process.

In our Western culture, we use the term "death" to describe endings in life that suggest finality. In my experience, when the soul leaves the body – the transformation from being embodied to being dis-embodied – is not final, so you will find that I have used other terms to replace the word "death." I invite you to be open to using other words for your loss, substituting the language with which you are most comfortable, and exploring how this impacts the nuances of your experience.

You will also see the word "beloved" used throughout the book in reference to your loved one whom you are grieving – whether this is your mother, father, brother, sister, child, animal companion, grandma, grandpa, aunt, uncle, neighbor, spouse, partner, lover, or friend. This is in alignment with the dictionary's definition of beloved as "a much loved person," not necessarily your lover or spouse. I prefer to use this word "beloved" because it is such a heartfelt word and describes the depth of relationship between two hearts and souls.

Finally, you can read this book any way you want to – from beginning to end, or you can just open to the section that draws you in and see what you discover.

If feelings arise for you as you read, please pause and feel them. Learning how to be with your self is far more important than reading the book.

By living with grief, you too could write your own book. Each survivor of loss is an author of a deep and moving story that includes heartache and transformation. Every person who experiences grief has a survivor's wisdom to share with others who are bereaved. Once we have lost a loved one, we share a common ground, a wound of loss, and this is why we are often referred to (or we call ourselves) "members of the club." The Club of Bereavement.

THE INEVITABLE MEMBERSHIP
INTO THE CLUB

One is either in this club or not.

I wish I weren't in this club – and I bet you have the same wish.

That's the thing with this club – none of us want to belong to it.

I dreaded membership into this club my whole life. As a matter of fact, before being initiated, I spent a lot of time contemplating how much I did *not* want to be part of this club.

That's how it is with grief. No one wants to be intimate with grief.

Yet, we are all destined to be. And not just once. But again and again...

We know that death is inevitable, and that we are actually in a relationship with death throughout all of life. Every moment of life, never to be experienced again. Every phase of life, never to be repeated. Yet, as pervasive as death is, we deny it, we rage at it, we call it unfair, we are consistently shocked by it, we resist it, we desperately don't want it – for ourselves or the ones we love. We also might flirt with it, tease it, beckon it and wish for it. Yet, even then, our response is often a screaming, "No, not now! Sometime, I know, but please, not now."

It rarely seems like the right time for someone we love to "die" – not for them, and certainly not for us. It is often shocking and traumatic, even when we are prepared for it.

None of us get away with living a life without grieving the ones we love.

Just by being born we are inevitable future members of the club.

There is a great story about the unavoidable and pervasive nature of grief:

The reputation of Buddha Shakyamuni had spread far and wide. Not only was he renowned as a great, compassionate and fully enlightened human being, but also as a skilled teacher and a miraculous healer who could even bring the dead back to life.

One day, a woman approached him after a teaching, begging that he do something to restore her dead child to her. The Buddha listened patiently to her plea and saw how great was her despair. He said to her, "Mother, if you bring me just one mustard seed from any household in which no person has died, then I shall revive your child."

The woman was greatly encouraged by the Teacher's words. She traveled from door to door throughout her own village, but could not find even a single residence in which no one had died. She went out of town, wandering to this hamlet and that in search of the tiny seed that the Buddha had requested. Days later, muddy and footsore, she returned to the place where the Buddha and his followers were passing the rainy season.

She was ushered into the Teacher's presence worn out, but not discouraged. "Master, try as I might, I could not locate the token you requested as an offering. But I have come to understand that death visits every household and eventually, every single one of us.

Inevitable, in every household.

My greatest wish is that this book will be a companion for you as you experience the nature of grief and find your way through this turbulent time.

THE NATURE OF GRIEF

1
"IT JUST SUCKS"

Don't tell me she had a good life.
Don't tell me it was a long life.
Don't tell me that there is a reason for everything.
Don't tell me she is in heaven.
Don't even tell me it will be okay in time.
Please, don't put a positive spin on my grief.
Because it just sucks. This is the bottom line.
There is no pretty pink ribbon for profound loss.
No lemonade.
No Band-Aid.
No pretty story that takes away the heartache of loss.

As the sinking reality sets in that you will not see or touch or smell your beloved again, the acute sense of loss can be like a sting that doesn't stop stinging; a heartache that keeps on aching; a nightmare that you can't wake up from.

Bottom line, loss is often traumatic. One of my clients described his tremendous grief for his wife in this way: "I don't know if I can bear it; it is intolerable. I don't know how I am going to take my next breath."

Loss also triggers a prevailing sense of loss of control that magnifies an experience of vulnerability that is actually always present but usually hidden from awareness in ordinary daily life. But denial is obviously interrupted when you can't stop death from taking your loved one and feelings are too overwhelming and raw to contain them. At any point in time, you might break into tears or be irritable, moody, angry or anxious.

You may wonder, "Will it suck forever?" The answer is yes and no. But for now, it helps to take it day-by-day, moment-by-moment.

Losing someone you love simply SUCKS.

As you reckon with how much it sucks, all you need to do is keep breathing.

2
RE-ARRANGED, NEVER THE SAME

Once you have experienced such deep loss, you aren't the same. Something happens. You are different. And you can't go back. An innocence is gone.

When loss occurred in my life, I called it "Stripped to the Core." Everything was different. I was different. Even my beliefs were impacted. Some of them were stripped away.

Grief is not something to be "worked through" as if it is a therapy issue. Rather, for now on, it is an ongoing, profound, and unavoidable, integral part of the experience of your life.

Life can be a strange ride when you are grieving. Moody, reactive, raw, lost, disoriented, and restless are just some of the many feelings associated with erratic behaviors such as waking up at strange hours of the early morning, breaking down into tears at unexpected moments, biting someone's head off when it's not quite warranted, not knowing what to do with yourself, not wanting to be with people, not wanting to be by yourself, walking around feeling empty and robotic, and on and on. You may feel like a stranger to your own self.

Just making it through a day in your life can be so challenging. People say they feel like they are "faking it," "pretending to be okay," and "trying to function as normally as possible."

Sometimes in the nature of grief, people are drawn to over-function. Check in with yourself. Are you pouring yourself into your work or parenting or cleaning the house as if your life depended on it? The act of absorbing yourself into something can feel like a lifeline, giving you a sense of purpose and focus, and might be the only way to feel like you can survive this time. Often, being busy with taking care of the estate or the beloved's belongings serves as the necessary distraction from what otherwise might feel like drowning in a ocean of grief.

Or, you may experience under-functioning. You might find that you cannot function at all, or can't handle nearly as much as you used to in a day. Sometimes people don't want to get out of bed and face the day. Driving can feel overwhelming. Going to work seems nearly impossible. You may feel aversion to what was your "normal" life, because you no longer identify with being the same person. But weirdly, your life still looks the same – except for this huge gaping hole.

After the loss of my mother, I knew I would never be the same. Most people I speak with feel exactly the same way. There is no going back. The broken glass can't be unbroken. Grieving yourself is part of the grieving process.

Of course, we continue to grow and heal. The trade-off, one that we would never sign up for, is that with our loss, we are given more awareness and acceptance of our vulnerability and mortality. In the wake of loss, we are often left with an intensity to live life fiercely and the fortitude to do so. It is all part of being undeniably re-arranged, never the same.

3
THERE IS NOTHING
LINEAR ABOUT GRIEVING

Grief doesn't just "get better with time," as if it's a straight road out of Dodge. Rather, the road spirals round and round with unexpected twists and turns. Those well-known, wonderful affirmations about how "it gets better and better every day" unfortunately do not apply to grief.

Grieving is just not that way.

You probably already have discovered this to be the case.

In the nature of grief, there is little control on when those twists and turns occur. Right when you may think you are *there* – "getting though it" or "making progress" – it is right then, at that precise moment of feeling relief, an unexpected twist or turn occurs and *bam*, you're back to feeling that deep heartache again that you thought you were past.

It's not your fault. You are not doing anything wrong.

Grief, by nature, isn't a direct line from A to Z.

Don't expect it to be. Expect the unexpected.

This is the nature of grief.

4
GRIEVING IS AN
INDIVIDUAL EXPERIENCE

No two people grieve alike. Every person is unique, with their own stories and individual styles of coping.

There is no correct way to grieve. There is no formula for grieving. You cannot dictate how the grieving process should go.

Grief is expressed in various ways. One person trembles and shakes, while another is numb. Some people start dating immediately after losing a spouse and marry soon after; while others isolate themselves and won't leave the house. Some people dive into work and become workaholics. Others can't focus on work so they take a leave of absence. Some people become scattered and foggy and others are hyper-focused on accomplishing tasks.

A client of mine said to me, "My husband died five years ago and I am still crying. What is wrong with me? My friend's husband passed away six months ago and she seems normal. She travels a lot and she has even gone out on some dates." Or, some might compare themselves to others in an attempt to feel better. Another client of mine said to me, "I think I am doing really great. I haven't cried for a few weeks and he just passed a few months ago. I know others who are still crying daily after two years."

The grief process cannot be compared. Every relationship is unique. One person might be grieving the love of her life and the other person might be grieving someone whom she was unhappy with and felt trapped by.

Either way, there is grief. When someone dies, they take with them the possibility for a closer relationship, the hope of ever resolving or healing interpersonal issues at some "future date." So, grieving a person you had "unfinished emotional business" with can be just as loaded – or even more so – than grieving someone with whom your communication was emotionally unfettered.

If your mind is doing this "compare, despair" thing, or "compare and make myself feel better" trip, just witness it, don't believe it, and don't fuel it. Comparing yourself to anyone doesn't heal anything.

5
THE FRONT BURNER, BACK BURNER PHENOMENON

One of my most frequently used metaphors to understand the nature of grief is that of a stove. The heartache of loss is either on the front burner or the back burner, but always on the burner.

When grief is on the back burner, the ache can often be felt but it is not at a screaming pitch, or running a lot of interference in your life at that moment. It is not ruling your emotions. You are able to be more in the present moment without the loss overshadowing everything you engage in.

When grief is on the front burner, it is the opposite. You are on fire with the ache, the longing, the burning. There is no escape; the grief colors everything.

One can only have grief be on the front burner for a certain amount of time without burning to a crisp. Allowing the shift to the back burner, or learning how to intentionally shift it to the back burner, is necessary for survival.

In time, you will have the experience of longer periods of time spent with the grief on the back burner.

Depending on the moment, sometimes you can move the intensity of grief to the back burner, and sometimes you cannot.

This is the Nature of Grief.

6
RIDING THE WAVES

When the experience of grief arises with intensity, it is experienced as a wave. "Riding the waves" is a common term used by club members. When the wave comes, it is often impossible to feel or do anything else than to ride it out. Just like when you are in the ocean and a wave is coming toward you, and it is clear that you can't stop that wave. It has a force to it. "Riding the waves" means that you allow for the intensity of the emotion to arise. You give yourself to it, you go with it, and you allow it to take you where it will, especially if you are in a safe space to do so.

Waves can catch you by surprise. You cannot always anticipate what will trigger a wave. Sometimes you may think a certain set of circumstances will trigger you and it doesn't. You can prepare for waves but to only some degree. What is important to keep in mind when a wave comes is that the intensity won't last forever.

It helps to hold onto a surfboard to ride the waves with. A surfboard can be many things. For some people, a surfboard may be faith or the support of family or communing with Nature. It can also be a mantra, rosary beads, or prayer. Sometimes it is a soothing thought that is intentionally repeated to get you through the intensity of the waves. Some examples of such thoughts are: "I can let myself feel this," "I am not going to drown," "This is happening and somehow I will survive this," or "It won't always feel this way."

Remember, riding the wave without drowning is all we are looking for.

Waves are expected to be intense in the beginning months of grief but they can also be surprisingly intense later on when you think they shouldn't be.

It is also okay to not always experience waves. Clients will sometimes report to me that they feel guilty if they are not always in pain after the loss of a loved one. They ask me if it is okay that sometimes they are not thinking about the loss and they might even be laughing and having a moment of reprieve. They ask me if it means that they really didn't love the person the way they should have.

It is natural for waves of grief to temporarily subside, to be spread apart and to arise again. Our physical, mental, and emotional bodies are not equipped to feel the intensity of grief at every moment.

It is not uncommon for a bereaved client to come into a session and report, "I am doing better this week."

I inquire, "What does this mean?"

"I haven't cried this week. I haven't had any big waves of grief."

This is the classic misunderstanding that one is doing "better."

I respond gently, "Actually this does not mean it is a 'better' week but rather, it is a week without tears. If you define yourself as doing 'better' when you aren't crying, then you will also judge yourself as doing 'worse' again when you have a week of tears, which will inevitably happen."

It is truly not a matter of doing "worse" or "better" in the nature of grief.

It is important not to get attached to any one phase of grieving as more okay than another. Grief is not to be judged. It is what it is. Judgment will only lead to more suffering. The nature of grief is that grief shows itself differently, from one day to the next, from hour to hour, from moment to moment.

Do you ever judge a wave when you are at the ocean and say, "That wave is okay but not that one?" Or, "The timing of that wave is wrong"? No, never, right? So, why judge your own waves of grief?

7
IMPERMANENCE IS AN ABSOLUTE

How many times do we hear the phrase, "Death is a part of life?" We know this. All of us know that we are going to die and everyone we love is going to die. It is the one absolute certainty in life that we are sure of. Yet, our reaction to death is usually one of shock, horror, devastating sorrow and resistance. We never seem to get use to this "death thing," although it is the one absolute inevitability in all of our lives.

At funerals, I find myself looking around at *all* of the faces in the congregation (older folks, babies, children, everyone...) and thinking, "Every one of us will have one of these." It is the way it is. Impermanence, unavoidable and undeniable. Each moment gives itself into the next, never to be lived again. Each phase of life dies into another, never to be repeated. The process of letting go is continuous, from the moment we are born. Moment by moment, hour by hour, day by day, week by week, month by month, season by season, year by year... it all passes.

I was leading a therapy group in which many of the clients were grieving their beloveds. It was a very sad night. At the close of the group, we sat close to one another, with tenderness and the intimacy that comes with sharing the experience of loss. The heartbeat of vulnerability was palpable as we sat together, close, tender and intimate in the shadow of death, acutely aware of fate. This word came to me to describe the experience of our mortality and I exclaimed, "We are all going to be *plucked!*" Everyone in the circle gasped. Plucked! The others agreed that it was the perfect word for what we were feeling. At some point, fate will swoop down on us, one at a time, and pluck us. I wondered to myself, "Is this how a chicken feels when a human hand grabs him and plucks his feathers? After the group dispersed, I looked up the word pluck in the dictionary. It gave several descriptions, some of which are: to eradicate, to be suddenly pulled with a jerk, to be moved by force, to snatch or rob, to be pulled out of a place of growth. Yes, the word fits! We have added the word to our vocabulary to express the finality that awaits.

The prevalence of death is in our face all day long – on the news, in the lives of our families and friends, and with the always-too-soon passing of our animal companions. Yet, somehow, no matter how much we know this, we continuously try to capture the fleeting moments to hold them still and remember them. We photograph them; we record them; we paint them; we sing them; we create poems and tell stories about them. We are inspired to create art as a way to make the moment into something more lasting.

SURRENDERING

8
SURRENDERING INTO GRIEF

During periods of grief, life has a surreal feeling to it. Time itself can be disorienting and confusing. Often people report that they wake up too early in the morning and they feel exhausted by the time they usually would get out of bed. I have heard the bereaved say that a decade can pass and the loss can seem like a year ago or a month ago. On the other hand, three months can pass since the death, and it can seem like ages ago that you held your beloved's hand.

The stages associated with the dying process are also experienced in grieving – denial, anger, bargaining, depression, and acceptance. You do not necessarily experience the stages in a linear order; rather, you can bounce from one to another daily and even experience several at the same time. As you are going through these stages, just know that it is normal, surrender into them, and live out the array of feelings and, in time, they will move through.

Reverberations of shock can remain for a long time. They are often experienced early in the morning, coming out of sleep, or when going to sleep. In the quiet hours, the harsh reality of loss has a way of pronouncing itself. Months and even years later, you might find yourself saying, "It is still soul-shocking! I can't believe I will never see him again."

Surrendering is the relinquishing of resistance. It is the act of yielding and submitting. The initial reaction to loss is often a screaming "NOOOO," yet even during that cry, there is a knowledge that all you really can do is surrender.

9
"GONE"

The biggest surrender is to the reality that your beloved is gone. Never to be seen, smelled, heard, or touched again.

The word "gone" is never more real than in the experience of death. How can it be true that this being that you love so much is now no longer here and never to be seen again? How is that?

It is a shocking, bizarre mixture of reality and unreality. With loss, the notion of never seeing the beloved again is often beyond the mind's grasp, and it can feel unreal, like a dream.

I remember calling the hospital room the day after my mom's surgery. Another woman's voice answered. I was taken back. I asked for my mom. The new occupant of the room said, "She's gone!"

I heard an inner alarm go off.

I will never forget her shrilling voice as she repeated, "She's gone."

And although, in actuality, she was not yet "gone", I knew in my gut that this was the beginning of the end.

After mom "died," I wrote in my journal:

Gone... yet I am always looking for her...

Gone... but I am always listening for her...

Gone... but I never stop longing for her...

The desire to be with her is never gone. Her body is gone – but her presence in my life is not gone and will never be. One of my biggest missions is to not allow her to be "gone." I look for ways to honor her, feel her, and include her in my life. I have continued to nurture myself in ways that she cared for me when I was a child. When I was sick, Mom used to rub Jean Nate perfume on my forehead. Even to this day when I am not feeling well, I find myself reaching for the Jean Nate bottle, even though I am no longer wild about the smell of it. I find myself quoting Mom to others and passing on her wonderful practical wisdom. I have even given two women's workshops on my mother's teachings! The relationship absolutely did not end with the death of her body.

What are the ways that you can keep your beloved's memory alive and make sure he or she is not gone from your life?

How "gone" is the beloved, really?

This question often opens the doorway for contemplating the mystery of what comes after death, beckoning people to deeply question and often go beyond their existing beliefs.

I am standing upon that foreshore. A ship at my side spreads her white sails in the morning breeze and starts for the blue ocean. She is an object of beauty and strength and I stand and watch her until at length she hangs like a speck of white cloud just where the sea and sky come down to mingle with each other. Then someone at my side says, "There! She's gone!" "Gone where?" "Gone from my sight, that's all." She is just as large in mast and spar and hull as ever she was when she left my side; just as able to bear her load of living freight to the place of her destination. Her diminished size is in me, not in her. And just at that moment when someone at my side says, "There! She's gone!" there are other eyes watching her coming and other voices ready to take up the glad shout, "Here she comes!"
— Bishop Brent, "The Unknown Shore"

10
LONGING IS YOUR NEW COMPANION

You may notice that as you grieve, the experience of longing may be your constant company. Longing is never so pronounced as in the experience of death. Longing aches. Longing is a visceral experience. You feel it in your body and the body never lies. Even with the clarity that longing doesn't bring the beloved back, even then, longing doesn't stop. That is because longing has nothing to do with cognitive understanding. Rather, longing arises from the heart.

People share with me in therapy how much they long to touch their beloved again, smell them, feel their touch, hear their laugh, and spend time with them. They can't get away from how much the heart aches and how much longing there is. I don't try to help my clients make the longing go away. Rather, the focus is to surrender into it, accept it, and embrace it as part of this new chapter in one's life.

People speak about the deep ache for one more day with their beloved, one more conversation, one more time to hold hands, one more time to feel the person's warm skin. This is how it is. People in grief would trade anything for "just one more..."

Bottom line, longing may be the companion that greets you first thing in the morning and may be the last to say goodnight to you.

Longing can grow to be so constant that it is perceived as the avenue for connection to the beloved. Then, when the longing subsides, one grieves for the longing, missing the company of it, feeling a bit lost and empty.

Longing is part of grieving – until it is not.

Eventually you will find other ways to feel close with your beloved.

All in time.

11
THE DOORWAY INTO VULNERABILITY

Up until now, you may have lived your life guarded by an elaborate defense system created to protect you from being "too vulnerable."

Grief does away with that. Vulnerability might as well now be your middle name, or possibly even your first name.

When vulnerable, the world is experienced differently. There is a softening, an openness, and sometimes a feeling of raw-ness. This might not exactly be comfortable. In fact, you might not like it at all. You might cry at everything. Or, you might be moody and reactive. Being vulnerable can feel like walking around in the world naked.

One of my bereaved clients experienced such an acute level of vulnerability that the sunlight was tormenting for her. The light of the day was too bright and felt too harsh to her raw heart. She covered up the windows with thick blinds and she didn't want to go out until night. The brightness of the day was diametrically opposed to what she felt within herself for the first six months after her brother died.

When my mom was in her descent, I was grateful that it was winter. I knew that if it was spring I would have to see people riding bikes, rollerblading, picnicking, and generally enjoying the warm weather. I didn't know how I would handle that. The gray skies and cold winds matched my insides. By the time she departed in March, I associated the beginning blossoms and emerging spring green with her re-birth that I was visualizing for her soul. On the day of her funeral, it was the most remarkable weather. As I looked up to the sky right before the service, I felt sun rays upon my face along with snowflakes and there above me was a rainbow!

Without the usual armor, there is a heightened awareness of everything. Observations, sensations, and synchronicity stand out as if they are printed in bold.

Vulnerability is an opening to the experience of universal suffering. Although you may feel alone in your pain, you may also experience a sense of unity with all beings – for all sentient beings suffer and experience loss.

In "normal" life, most of us have enough armor so that we can read about tragedies in the news and simultaneously eat lunch. We can work out at our fitness clubs as we watch the news about the daily horrors and we just keep running or biking or lifting weights. We are exposed to something horrible and then the next moment, we turn around and enthusiastically greet a friend. Our everyday living calls for a certain degree of dissociation and detachment at all times.

But when in grief, life is not "normal" as usual, and the new MO is a far cry from a detached stance. The horror you watch on the news may stay with you all day. You cry over disturbing emails about global suffering and atrocities and the greed that doesn't allow for solutions. The line that once separated your suffering from others' suffering has become blurred. Grief allows for the awareness that we are truly not separate from one another.

If your experience of grief leads you to this door, walk through it without hesitation, even if it immensely hurts. Herein lies the sacred.

12
WHEN DEATH IS UNEXPECTED

"I was with her this morning as she got dressed and ready for the day, like any other day. I had no idea it was the last time I would see her - the last day of her life!"

"I just spoke to him an hour before..."

"We had plans for this weekend..."

"We were going on a trip together..."

"We were supposed to meet at the coffee shop and I thought it was weird when I didn't hear from him..."

"She didn't come home from work. We were going to have an evening home together, cuddling and watching our favorite shows..."

"We just met for lunch..."

"We were sharing notes in the meeting today..."

"She was so vital... so healthy... so engaged... so..."

"How could this be true? How could this be real?"

"NOOOOOOOOOOOOO!

It can't be true! NOOOOOOOOOOOOOOOOOOOO!"

Does any of this sound familiar? Nothing is more shocking than unexpected death. It is pure trauma to every cell of the body.

If this is your reality, I am so sorry. There is no way around this painful shock. When death is sudden, it magnifies the word "surrender" like nothing else and there is nothing else to do but to go through it.

Expect yourself to go in and out of denial and shock. It doesn't just occur in the beginning. Expect yourself to feel anger – more anger than you have ever known. Expect despair, depression, and anxiety. Expect thinking and feeling all the worst stuff you can possibly imagine about the unfairness of life and death and God. Expect to have thoughts like "Why couldn't you have taken me instead" and "I'd do anything for this not to be true" as well as "I don't want to be here!" and "What is the point of living if this is what it comes to?" and "What were the last moments like?" Expect it all.

If death has occurred unexpectedly, you are in trauma. You cannot expect anything else from yourself but to keep your head above water (most of the time) and to just keep breathing. Unexpected death and loss is one of the biggest shocks to the body and one of the worst things that can happen.

Healing from PTSD (Post Trauma Stress Disorder) takes a long time. This disorder manifests in symptoms such as not being able to sleep, having anxiety, engaging in self-destructive behaviors, isolating, depression, impulsive high-risk adventures and an overall sense of feeling crazy. PTSD results in hormonal and other biochemical shifts that are quite real. When your primal brain goes into action, your cortisol levels increase, your serotonin levels decrease, your dopamine is suppressed, and you probably will feel anxious, depressed, unable to sleep, or unable to function in some way. It is important to understand these physiological changes so that you can have more compassion and patience for yourself and be more informed on how to manage it.

Don't go through it alone. Enlist professional therapeutic support. By having a professional guide, you are provided a safe place to express your feelings and to learn coping skills for dealing with your new unwanted reality. Therapeutic support may even help you to connect with an aspect of yourself that remains intact, beneath it all.

With unexpected trauma, many times people resist the healing and recovery process. They don't want to move on. They think that if they become "okay," then they are condoning what happened. But because it wasn't okay, they won't let themselves feel okay. This kind of thinking is part of the trauma of loss.

It will change in time, whether we believe we want it to or not.

13
WHEN SUICIDE HAPPENS

The person who completes suicide, dies once. Those left behind die a thousand deaths, trying to relive those terrible moments and understand... Why? — Clark

The devastating trauma of suicide is a nightmare. Shock waves reverberate for a long time to come. Along with murder, it may be the harshest experience of loss in life.

Every possible feeling that is involved in the grieving process is magnified a thousand fold when a beloved dies from suicide. Soul shock, anger, rage, guilt, regrets, sadness, depression, horror, agony, emptiness are all intensified.

Every person closely connected to the person who dies from suicide tends to feel responsible. *What could I have done differently? Why didn't I...? If only I had been there. If only I hadn't allowed her to be alone! I should have known. I should have gotten help for him. I only wish I had... I will be haunted by this regret forever. I am being punished. I wish I could rewind time...*

The mind goes over and over the last few days of the beloved's life, searching for any clues or indications that this was going to happen – and ruminating about how it could have been prevented. Every person has their own version of what they could have done differently. Self-blame is a very common obsession for survivors.

Besides self-blame, survivors often feel abandoned. In a typical conversation with a survivor, I said to someone who lost her father to suicide: "You know, he loved you very deeply." She quickly responded with, "Well, obviously, not deeply enough."

Believing that someone's love for you is lacking because they died of suicide is personalizing something that is not personal. You wouldn't personalize someone having a heart attack or someone dying of cancer. The personal pain that drives a person to suicide is as much a symptom of a disease process as is any other symptom of any other illness that is out of one's control and can lead to death.

But because suicide appears to be a choice, different from a heart attack, it adds to the harshness of the abrupt loss. Yet, in ways, it is just like a heart attack. The heart is attacked with a brutal experience of life and it can't take it any longer. There is a mystery to suicide that will never be understood – one will never know *exactly* what the person was going through that allowed this to happen.

You can't stop the mind from having self-destructive and blaming thoughts – but they do nothing good. These thoughts only hurt you even more. You are already experiencing such devastation; you do not need any more. You cannot help having these thoughts, but you can choose not to fuel them.

Instead, practice witnessing them and just gently make the sound *Shhhhh*, like a mother makes when rocking her child. The sound itself soothes and quiets the mind. Try it. Take a deep inhale, and with a long exhale, make the sound *Shhhh*. Notice what happens. Do it a few times. Experiment with closing your eyes and making the sound. Again, just notice... The sound *Shhhhh* quiets the mind and is much more effective than trying to force "positive thoughts."

It is important to not isolate and go into hiding. Share with people close to you. Let a professional therapist help you. Forgiveness is a must. No matter what you did or didn't do, you can not possibly be the cause for the suicide. It is not your fault.

I am of the belief that if a person has a destiny with suicide, they will eventually find their way to it. Even people who are hospitalized in locked wards find a way to end their lives if that is what they really want to do.

Anger is normal with any loss, but especially with suicide. Although we know that the loved one did not have the resources to do anything else than to end the pain in this way, anger still arises. The anguished questions come in waves, such as: "How could you do this to me?" "How could you do this to your children?" "How could you be so selfish?" "How could you abandon us?"

You must allow these questions and not judge yourself for anything that you feel. Rage, despair, hopelessness, and self-destructive impulses are all part of the trauma. Reckoning with the pain and imagining the sense of aloneness that the beloved must have experienced is gut-

23

wrenching, tormenting, and unavoidable.

Surviving suicide of a beloved is so difficult. The grief hurts horribly and haunts one like nothing else. There is no way around it. You have to go through it in order to survive. The experience of guilt is also intensified. The anger is turned inward and beats you up with accusations like "How could I have not seen this? Why didn't I...?" Of course, these self-attacking questions only cause further suffering and often arise as a desperate attempt to avoid feeling completely out-of-control in regard to this tragic event.

You may feel like hiding and not wanting to be seen by others. Be around those you feel safe with. Be honest about what happened. It is not your fault or a poor reflection on you – or your beloved. You may think people blame you. They usually do not. And should not. Judgment arises from uneducated, misinformed understanding based in fear. More often than judgment, there is usually immense compassion and sorrow for survivors. Experiment with looking in the eyes of those who approach you. Practice receiving the love and support that everyone wants to give to you. You are the only one who can know how much you can take in. Pace yourself. Take time to rest. You must rest. You are in trauma.

Often you may feel physically sick. The body, mind, and heart are one. You need help and support for the care of every level of you. Don't hesitate to seek help. There are many survivors and survival groups as well as organizations dedicated to helping you.

Keep a daily journal of your thoughts and feelings. Learn to be with yourself in this time. Practice saying the word "suicide" out loud to let your self know that there is nothing to be ashamed of. Soothe yourself. You deserve for your mind to be gentle with yourself – to be your own ally, not your foe.

Remember, experiencing a beloved die from suicide is one of the most intense traumas a person can experience and thus, calls for the utmost of patience.

14
EVERY LOSS BRINGS US CLOSER
TO OUR OWN MORTALITY

Our perception of death causes us to contract in some way when we hear about it or see it. Often the news of a death is experienced as truly shocking to the nervous system, whether it is the death of a movie star, a political figure, or of course, someone we are close to. Bottom line, death is almost always distressing. Yet, death is the only guaranteed experience we all have in life, besides breathing and the fact that life is change.

A client recently wrote to me about his grieving process, in which he described how grief is bringing him face to face with his own death:

Yes, I miss Susan and my parents. This has been a series of traumatizing losses, but it is my own mortality that has me grief stricken and truly befuddled. Yes, I have been undone by the grief that has accompanied the deaths of those I have loved so helplessly, and I am terrified of losing more dear friends and family. Yet, as devastating as all this is and will be, and it is and will be unknowably unbearable, it is mostly foreshadowing of that which is most horrific: I'm going to join them.

With loss of the beloved, mortality becomes vividly real. For the first few years after Mom's departure, I was so tuned into grief that I was obsessed with the thought that one day I will say goodbye to everyone I love – including me.

This is not necessarily a bad thing. Carlos Castaneda emphasized in his classic book, *The Teachings of Don Juan,* the importance of having death in your awareness at all times. He says this about death:

Think of your death now. It is at arm's length. It may tap you any moment, so really you have no time for crappy thoughts and moods. None of us have time for that. The only thing that counts is action, acting instead of talking.
You have to be aware of the uselessness of your self-importance and of your personal history. Your death can give you a little warning, it always comes as a chill. Death is our eternal companion, it is always to our left, at an arm's length.

How can anyone feel so important when we know that death is stalking us? The thing to do when you're impatient is to turn to your left and ask advice from your death. An immense amount of pettiness is dropped if your death makes a gesture to you, or if you catch a glimpse of it, or if you just have the feeling that your companion is there watching you.
The issue of our death is never pressed far enough. Whenever you feel that everything is going wrong and you're about to be annihilated, turn to your death and ask if that is so. Your death will tell you that you're wrong; that nothing really matters outside its touch. Your death will tell you, "I haven't touched you yet." Death is the only wise adviser that we have.

Through the awareness of death "to the left of you," you are given the gift to relish the present moment, the only moment you have.

THE MENTAL GYMNASTICS
OF THE GRIEVING MIND

15
"IF ONLY... IF ONLY... WHAT IF..."

The mind has a tendency to obsess with thoughts that start with the haunting words "What if" and "If only." These thoughts repeat over and over, sometimes finishing with different answers, sometimes the same answer. It helps to understand that this is just what the mind does and nearly everyone engages in it for a while after a loss. Regrets are unavoidable.

There is a certain pull, experienced like an undertow, for the mind to ruminate on what it can't control, but believes it could, if only...

Regrets tell you that if you had done something differently, the result would have been altered. Unfortunately, this tendency of the mind adds insult to injury and causes deep suffering.

The mind will obsess like this for a while because it is set on believing that it is more powerful than it is. It is invested in believing that it could have impacted the course of how life unfolded. "If only I had left later, if only I had called her, if only I had been there, if only I had told her to take a left when we got to the corner instead of going straight, if only I had slept over that night and she hadn't been alone, if only we chose the other medical treatment..."

The "if only" and "what if" patterns of thinking are endless loops of unnecessary suffering. They are fabricated stories that ultimately don't serve any purpose except to make you feel bad. They do not serve to bring clarity. They do not bring resolution or peace.

But the mind insists on engaging in this painful exercise anyway. The only function this obsessive pattern of thinking serves is self-punishment, as if the suffering from the loss is not enough.

These mental gymnastics that cause "unnecessary suffering" are actually a distraction from the deep and real suffering of the loss. Self-blame and pondering how it could have been different can be less confrontational than the remaining void caused by the loss.

Allow these thoughts to move through you like storms. But be forewarned — they won't lead you anywhere. They loop round and round and only make you feel worse. My advice is to practice observing your mind. Dim your awareness of it, allowing it to be in the background as if it is white noise. Do not invest belief in its story. The saying "Don't believe everything your mind thinks" certainly applies here. These obsessive patterns of thinking are painful, so painful, senseless, and untrue. It is the ego arguing with reality, which leads nowhere.

How to limit this obsessive thinking? Have a conversation with your mind just like you would set limits with a child for his or her own good. You can contract with it and give it time allotments to tell it, "Okay, Mind, have at it, go wild with all the *what if*s and *if only*s you can possibly think of. Let's dump them all out for the next five minutes and then that's it for now. No more! Dear Mind, you can do this twice a day for a while. But if you try doing it at other times, I am going to swat at you like you are a fly and I won't pay attention to you at all." (Well, you wouldn't say that last sentence to a child but it's completely reasonable to say it to the mind when it is beating you up.)

As time passes, you will probably not be as bombarded by the regrets. You can change your contract for "dumping" to once a day and then every other day, then once a week to once a month to, hopefully, very rarely, if ever. This technique of "contracting" with the negativity is a way of taming the mind and not allowing it to take you in whatever direction it comes up with. It is a way of protecting yourself from the self-berating, obsessive thinking that causes only unnecessary suffering.

16
"I JUST WANT HER BACK..."

This is another form of mind gymnastics, arising from longing, repeated over and over as if it might have the power to change things. This is exactly what my 38-year-old client grieving her mother said to me: "If I say how much I want her back often enough, I believe somewhere inside of myself that maybe... just maybe... it will bring her back." This thought becomes a connector to the beloved. People are also afraid *not* to feel this anymore, another level of letting go. Either way, it is all part of the grieving process – and all stages of the grieving process are to be experienced, even though they hurt so much

There are steps to take to help you work with obsessive thoughts. First, observe your mind. Then, name what your mind is doing. For example: "My mind is stuck on wanting her back."

Then, ask yourself, "Is this serving me?" Just asking this question reminds you there is another part of you available besides the thoughts that are swirling around and hurting you. This part of the self can be a witness to the pain rather than be overwhelmed by it.

If you believe your mind is saying something that is important for you to focus on, ask yourself, "Is this the best time for me to be thinking about this?" For example, it might not be the best thing to be going on in your mind while you are at work.

If the answer is "yes," then give yourself fully to it in such a way that is meaningful to you, whether it is to write about it, talk about it, chart it out, or deeply engage with it in some way. If the answer is "no," which is more often the case, then learn to soothe the mind by gently saying to it, "Dear Mind, let's not do this now. It is not serving us." Then, give your mind something else to focus on that will serve you in the present moment.

17
REMORSE

The dictionary defines remorse as deep and painful regret for wrongdoing; compunction.

Few people bypass the gnawing, gut-wrenching, haunting experience of remorse.

It is important to discern between the experience of genuine remorse rather than lamenting over "perceived failures." In remorse, there are tears of humility and a surrendering to the knowingness that you would show up differently today than you did then. Remorse is embedded with deep heartfelt sorrow, beckoning forgiveness.

This is different than focusing on *perceived* failures. The critical mind gravitates to finding "what you did wrong" and mulls it over again and again. This kind of regret is a different experience than the sorrow of genuine remorse. It feels more like a mental clobbering and attack, rather than heartache. It can not lead to forgiveness because it is not based on the truth of a real wrongdoing but rather on a narrative that has been concocted to be punishing and distracting.

The mind can usually find something to regret – the missed opportunities to show up and express love. The list may include the last time you canceled your time together, not calling enough, not visiting enough, not saying "I love you" enough, being angry with her the last time you saw her, etc. These regrets are real, as well as unavoidable. Everyone feels them – yet they are not useful for healing.

How can we love enough and express our love to everyone fully, all the time? It's impossible. How can you expect yourself to love perfectly? This is also impossible.

How could you not have regrets and remorse? Again, impossible. The fact is that they are baked into the cake of every relationship.

18
OBSESSING ABOUT THE LAST MOMENTS

The mind often gets stuck thinking obsessively about the last days or hours of the beloved's life. If you were present during the last days of the beloved's life, the mind will often replay the dying process over and over. Frequently, I hear people say, "I can't get it out of my mind."

If you weren't with the beloved at the time of death and it happened suddenly and abruptly, the mind will ruminate over what the beloved experienced. It is pure anguish to not know the exact details and become preoccupied with the unknown and unknowable. This adds tremendously to the suffering of the one who grieves.

Why is it that the mind deliberates over the last days or moments of the beloved's life when there is so much more to a lifetime?

It might be the factor of not having control that drives the mind crazy. It might be in our hard-wiring to want to reduce the suffering of those we love, even if this leaves us banging against the wall of powerlessness and hopelessness. It might be the reverberations of shock from trauma and a splintered psyche that is trying to find a sense of resolution.

Bereaved clients have also shared with me that by ruminating about the last moments of their beloved's life, they believe they will somehow magically make it different.

Other people have stated to me that they feel guilty – known as "survivor's guilt" – and that by focusing on the last moments, they feel a sense of necessary punishment.

Another factor that feeds obsessive thinking about the last moments is that they weren't there with the beloved when it happened and the mind cannot get away from the pain of leaving something so unresolved.

In the depths of pain, we gravitate to the darkness. Despair has its own gravitational pull – a life of its own – further plummeting us into despondency. In this hole, everything is perceived through a disheartened lens that furthers our sadness and sense of loss. Obsessions about the very end of the beloved's life can be some of the darkest material the mind can come up with, effectively intensifying the pain and grief you feel.

Yet, the truth is that your beloved is no longer suffering. What happened is "history" for your beloved. *You* are the one who is suffering and your mind is keeping the suffering alive.

If your mind is haunted by the ending for your beloved, ask yourself: "What am I seeking through this obsession? What am I trying to resolve? How is this focus (perhaps perversely) serving me? What is it costing me?"

Seek beneath the obsession and find out what is motivating your obsessive thinking. Is it remorse? Guilt? Sorrow? Go under the obsessive thought pattern to the unresolved feelings that are perpetuating it. Be compassionate with yourself and gently move towards healing avenues for resolving what feels raw and unfinished.

19
UNFINISHED BUSINESS

With grief, unresolved issues that you didn't even know still existed may unexpectedly come to the surface.

If you don't feel good enough, if you don't feel worthy, if you don't feel confident, if you get anxious in response to change, or if you tend to use substances when you are stressed, this is the time that the ghosts come out of the closet. A bereaved 64-year-old client of mine who had accomplished a tremendous amount of therapy work lost his wife, the love of his life, two years ago. In his slow journey back to connecting with other women, he was shocked to confront old pain and insecure feelings he thought were long gone decades ago. BAM! There they were again! This is the power of grief.

Surviving loss often leads to big transformations – career changes, geographic moves, travel adventures, returning back to school, and manifesting certain dreams into realities. It is often recommended to hold off on making big decisions after a loss or any tragedy, due to the very fact that trauma can trigger biochemical changes that can cloud vision and make it more difficult to understand long-term consequences of a decision.

Also accompanying loss are changes in family dynamics. Unresolved issues in the family system push to the surface, calling out for attention. Although family members may have fewer resources than usual to deal with these issues, it is also a powerful time for healing old wounds. Grief softens the defense mechanisms that usually keep the status quo going, which opens the door for opportunities to be more honest and to open hearts and be compassionate with one another.

Loss also impacts friendships. Unexpected shifts can occur – some friends that you thought would be there don't show up and other friends come through that you wouldn't have predicted. Like a deck of cards thrown up into the air, every card lands in a different spot. This is the nature of grief – everything changes.

ONE LOSS BRINGS UP ALL LOSS

In the nature of grief, there is often a flooding of memories of other losses. Whether the memories are conscious or not, the pain from other times of loss are often experienced with the new loss. This is because they are all stored in the same place – the heart.

The heart has limitless "RAM" – endless access to the feelings of all of the losses one has lived through. For example, a young woman's gushing tears from a breakup with her boyfriend are probably also about missing her dad who died a few years ago, and longing for her estranged brother who was very close to her in childhood. Experiencing loss of your beloved might lead you to missing the sweet company of your dog who was such a comfort to you. The examples are endless. What is important to know is that, although it might not make sense to the rational mind, and you might not even have insight into all that you are grieving, one loss brings up other losses.

As we inevitably accumulate loss in a lifetime, the feelings are not only in our conscious mind but also tucked in the subconscious and unconscious crevices of the mind. In order to survive the devastating nature of loss and live with the reality of impermanence, we automatically suppress feelings.

Being out of touch with our feelings does not mean they are gone. They are stored in our cells and are referred to as "cellular memory," which is outside of one's conscious daily awareness. In our normal living, we develop effective defense mechanisms to block pain so that we can enjoy our lives. However, the trauma of losing a beloved has the power to shock the nervous system, pierce through our defenses, and expose the tender wound of all losses: past, present, and even anticipated losses in the future.

The grieving process offers an opportunity to experience what was suppressed and perhaps waiting for your attention. You don't have to understand all that you are grieving. No need to analyze it. Just allow – and the river of grief will take you where you need to go.

21
THE GRIEF CHANNEL

In the grieving process, one can get stuck in the experience of loss. Everything in life might be experienced through the lens of what I call "the grief channel."

Examples of this that I have heard from my bereaved clients are as follows:

"As I touch the skin of my loved ones who are still here with me, I wonder when I will lose them."

"As I was gathering my things on the plane once it landed, I looked around and saw everyone as skeletons."

"I can hear the tick-tock of my own life on a loud speaker. How many full moons are left for me to see?"

"I can't stop wondering how many nights of sleeping by my husband's side I have left."

"I watch children with their parents, and I think about how they will lose their parents one day too and feel orphaned like I do."

When tuned into "the grief channel," the usual filters and defenses lessen and the experience of pervasive loss overrides everything else. Awareness of impermanence permeates every experience. Being attuned to the suffering all around the world may increase dramatically. There is a gift to this level of connection, as it brings you deeper into your heart of compassion.

22
HOW MORTALITY IMPACTS LOVING

Standing face to face with the fact that we are going to "die" opens us to the possibility of wholeheartedly loving life right now, as it is. This kind of awakening beckons the heart to open and allows for an unconditional acceptance of our loved ones. Do you notice that people don't ask their loved ones in their final days to change or improve in some way? This is when most of us finally give up wanting others to be different. Instead, in the face of death, the universal inclination is to embrace the loved one just as he or she is.

Just imagine living this way before we are confronted with losing our loved ones.

A common spiritual practice is to contemplate death as a way to deepen a sense of gratitude for being alive in the present moment. But little attention is given to the impact that our fears of loss have on how much we allow ourselves to love. There is often a tendency to hold ourselves back, consciously or unconsciously, from loving because we are so afraid to lose that person one day. And we subconsciously think it will hurt a little less if we don't give ourselves fully to love.

I have heard this many times from clients when they finally allow themselves to feel deeply connected with someone. After all the many issues couples work through, this becomes the bottom line – living with the knowingness that the day will come when they will have to say goodbye to one another. Bottom line, mortality influences how vulnerable we allow ourselves to feel.

How deeply can you let go into loving someone without awareness of the fear of losing them?

The fear can go underground and find ways of disrupting the flow of love. Most of us, from early dysfunctional family dynamics, are trained, consciously or unconsciously, in the art sabotaging deep connection. This level of drama creates a familiar sense of distance. Most people do not associate the dynamics that cause distance with fear of mortality, yet with further investigation, it is often the bottom line.

It is nearly impossible to talk oneself out of fear. If you feel anxiety about losing your beloveds, try this spiritual practice: Imagine the fear as a channel, just like on TV. The channel is based on finiteness, fear of loss, and negative predictions.

Now, change the channel. Try being aware of your "light body" that permeates the physical body with its life energy. The "light body" does not terminate with the physical body when it dies. It is known to not have endings or beginnings; rather it is endless and eternal. It is energy. Energy only transforms, it does not expire.

Invite yourself to at least be curious about the "light body," even if you don't have experiences of it.

Here is a demonstration of an experience of switching channels: As my husband and I are holding each other, the love is so palpable that we experience a sense of oneness – for a moment. In the next moment, fear reminds me that I will lose him one day. I try everything I know to come back to our sense of unity. I attempt to talk myself out of thinking thoughts about the future but to no avail. I intentionally intensify sensory input from my senses; this is usually effective to get me out of my head and bring me more into the present moment. I focus on the sensations in my body as his strong arms hold me tight. But I must admit that I can still feel some anxiety connected to the awareness of mortality. So, I intentionally change channels – from our personality and physical selves to the limitless energy that animates our physical bodies. I call this our "light bodies." As I do this, I sense a transcending of our mortal selves into energy that does not die with our bodies. Now, I am freer to melt into him, without anxiety.

This is a spiritual "practice," a positive experience of "mental gymnastics." The pull to identify with the physical body and your personality self is powerful. It is like a trance and is extremely difficult to interrupt. So, simply keep practicing shifting your identification from your physical body to your "light body."

One definition of happiness is living without fear. As I pondered how to be happy in the face of mortality, I had a dream or visit from Chris, my brother-in-law who recently died from AIDS. Before he departed, he had told me about long slender figures of light he had met in a near-death experience. In this dream, I found myself surrounded by the beings of light he had described to me. They gathered around me in a circle and they were so beautiful and loving. Their words reached into my heart: *We are the reason for your happiness.*

Light beings. I believe we are all light beings, dressed up in our bodies and personalities like costumes. Then we inevitably forget we are the light and actually believe we are these costumes.

What if we practiced remembering more often?

If we practice seeing ourselves through a spiritual lens, maybe, just maybe, we might be able to access this channel a little bit more easily when we are confronted with loss.

HOW TO NAVIGATE
THROUGH GRIEF

23
MAKING IT THROUGH A DAY

In the nature of grief, functioning can be challenging – sometimes *very* challenging. Be compassionate with yourself. Commit to doing the baseline of self-care. Think of yourself as your own parent. *Let's get out of bed, brush your teeth, wash your face, get dressed, and eat something.* Be gentle yet encouraging with each step you take. Good parents, even in times of crisis, won't abandon their children and leave them to fend for themselves.

Live into the day, moment by moment. Step by step. Inhale and exhale. Breath by breath. Just do the next thing, and if possible, the next *loving* thing, and then the next loving thing. Allow for naps or rest from the busyness of the day. In grief, everything can seem overwhelming, over-stimulating, challenging and exhausting. Tasks can take much longer and be harder to complete. Paperwork can pile up and the thought of doing laundry can seem like climbing a mountain. Brain chemistry is strained from trauma, so everything is more difficult. Just do the next thing. Be kind to yourself. Patient and tender.

It won't always be like this. Breathe into it. Shamelessly ask for help. It's important to allow others to be there with you.

Allow the tears when they arise. Include distractions into your day to give yourself a break, like reading a novel or watching a movie. If you are feeling "not yourself" (foggy, numb, reactive, negative, depressed, irritable, emotional, or unproductive), it might mean that your emotional pipes are clogged with unfelt feelings.

To unclog the build-up of gunk in the pipes, take time daily for your grieving process and schedule in daily self-care. Be committed to this self-care time, no matter what. Ask yourself, "What would feel nurturing to me right now?" And then do it. Through loving attention and action, show yourself that you matter.

24

GIVE PERMISSION TO ALL
OF YOUR FEELINGS

To "give permission" means to allow, to give way to, to surrender, to not resist or fight, and to let go of judgment.

Giving permission is different than acceptance. The concept of acceptance insinuates a sense of embracing and being at peace. Giving permission does not necessarily imply feeling peaceful or embracing. It means saying "yes" to exactly where you are and what you are experiencing. It is about surrendering into what is occurring, including the experience of resistance and *not* being at peace.

Permission-giving is a moment-to-moment spiritual practice that calls for being kind to yourself. It is a practice that gives permission to whatever feelings arise: anger, discouragement, sorrow, heartache, heartbreak, guilt, pleasure, anxiety, fear. *The guiding rule is to never make yourself wrong for anything that you feel.* Besides, making yourself wrong does not make the feeling stop – it only intensifies it. Remember, what you resist *persists*.

Grieving is an emotional roller coaster ride. It is important to be discerning about when to fully express your feelings. If you are not in a safe and appropriate setting, then acknowledge the feelings, internally give them permission, and bracket expressing them to another time.

Sometimes, as intense feelings arise, you might need someone to be with you and hold you. Learn to ask for what you need. If you are alone, create a sense of being held and contained by wrapping yourself tightly with a blanket or shawl. It's okay to allow shaking, sobbing and longing to be expressed. It doesn't mean you are "losing it" if you shake and wail.

The depth of feeling that comes with loss cannot be underestimated. With grieving, it is not necessarily true that just "having a good cry" will bring relief as if does for other situations in life.

In grief, the intention is not necessarily to "feel better," but rather to be true to the process, and to allow it to be fully what it is and you to be as you are.

Please make note that giving permission to feelings is *not* the same as giving permission to acting out destructive or self-destructive behaviors. This is a very important distinction. No matter how much you might hurt, it is not okay to hurt yourself or someone else in any way.

Giving permission to your feelings can serve as an antidote to depression, which is often caused by the suppression of feelings. When feelings are pushed down, they can turn into a low-grade chronic depressive state called dysthymia, or if they are ignored long enough, they can manifest as an acute clinical depression.

As you allow your feelings, you experience your authentic self. Even if it feels like your heart is breaking, living true to your heart will ultimately heal you.

25
LET OTHERS KNOW YOU ARE "GRIEVING"

What do you say when people ask you, "How are you?" and you know that all that is really happening for you is grief and disorientation? You can simply respond with the one word that says it all: "Grieving." This one word explains why you may sometimes feel anxious for no reason at all, or angry and irritable, or overwhelmed and frustrated, or why you may break down in tears, or why you sometimes feel lost and numb, or disoriented and restless. This one word says, "This is not a normal time in my life – and it will never be 'normal' again in the same way. I am grieving my loved one. I am grieving myself. I am grieving the life and world I knew." Letting people know what is real for you is an invitation for authentic connecting.

Many people in bereavement report that as time goes by, others relate to them as if they are the same as before the loss. This discrepancy of how people see them and how they feel inside can actually worsen with the passing of time. Sometimes the bereaved person experiences expectations that they naturally should feel "better" since time is moving on. In response to this expectation, the inclination is to go underground with the grief and to cover it up with a front of normalcy. The experience of ongoing grief can breed shame based on the belief that one should be "over it." This inauthenticity intensifies a sense of separation and isolation. One of my clients, who lost her beloved ten years earlier, confided to me that she still grieves her husband daily. She expressed huge relief when I let her know that grief doesn't necessarily ever leave and there was nothing abnormal about her grieving process.

Often people close to those grieving may think they are being supportive of the bereaved by reinforcing that they should be moving on. "It's been three years, right? What are you doing now?" Or, they may not mention the loss in hopes to not remind you of it or bring you down. Or, they just may not be thinking about your grief at that moment. We all have our denial mechanisms to minimize the depth and impact of loss.

Whatever may be the case, be as forthright and authentic as you can be, which gives you the best chance to feel connected to others. Next time someone asks you how you are, experiment with responding with this one word – "grieving" – and see if it feels better than saying, "I'm okay" when you aren't feeling okay.

26
YOU CAN'T TELL GRIEF TO GO AWAY
BUT YOU CAN LEARN TO "BRACKET" IT

You can't tell grief, "No more. I am tired of you so go away." But it is possible to learn to "bracket" feelings. By bracketing, I mean contracting with your self to contain the experience of grief for another time and putting it on the back burner. It can be as simple as stating to your grief, "Let's put you on the back burner for now and I promise to bring you to the front burner when I get home."

The skill of bracketing is often necessary for functioning in the world. However, it is only effective if you commit to attending to the bracketed feelings by creating a safe space to feel them, and it is usually best to do this within the same twenty-four hour period of time.

The practice of bracketing will either strengthen or weaken your trust in yourself. What you do with your bracketed feelings will inevitably impact how you feel with yourself. If you don't make time for the bracketed feelings, then it's a guarantee that you won't feel right with yourself in some way and your functioning will eventually be hindered.

It can be challenging to return to the feelings once they are bracketed. People often share that they have a hard time accessing the feelings later in the day once the feelings are effectively bracketed – or, they simply don't want to. The truth is that these feelings will arise again, even if you try to avoid them. But they might arise at inappropriate times with fierce intensity.

By creating time to be with your grief, you may lessen the onslaught of unwanted triggers, but more significantly, you will also deepen the trust in yourself that you will take care of yourself in this turbulent time.

So, make time to be with your grief, to intentionally bring it to the front burner. Even if you aren't feeling the intensity of the feelings, they are still there. Even if you don't want to follow through, remember that you made a commitment to yourself and it is important to keep your word to yourself. If the feelings aren't naturally arising in the time period that you designated to be with your grief, you can enter into it by writing about what it was like to feel them earlier.

The nature of grief calls for quality time and attention.

27
WAYS TO SPEND TIME
WITH THE GRIEF

Create safe spaces and times to be with yourself and your feelings. Time to be with your tears and anguish. Time to have conversations with your loved one, even if they are one-way conversations. Time to feel your longing and your heartache, and time to remember. A safe space is a place where you feel free to express your emotions out loud, uninterrupted. No phone calls, no children or animals to care for, no one else to attend to – just you with you.

Create time to journal on a daily basis as a way to commune with your internal emotional life. In the book *The Artist's Way*, Julia Cameron recommends that you write three pages every day, without necessarily having an agenda of what you are going to say. You just bring your pen to paper and write... and write some more... until you fill up the three pages. This gives an opportunity to spill out on paper the contents of your mind and for your heart stirrings to make themselves known. Often insights arise that you didn't know were there.

I call my journals "Conversations with Momsy." I am now on my fifth one. Writing letters to my mom offers comfort as well as a direct way to spend time with my grief process – and perhaps the most significant impact is that it has provided a way for me to continue to experience our talks.

Create rituals in your life as a way to channel your pain into meaning. The word "ritual" means to externalize your inner world in some way that feels sacred, to act out something that feels meaningful, and then to bring it back inside of yourself.

Opportunities to engage in ritual can occur spontaneously. More often, however, they occur through intention and making time for it. A first step toward creating a ritual is pausing in a busy life to contemplate what your ritual would be.

I created an altar in my bedroom that is dedicated to honoring my mom. It is a lovely spot by the window so it is brightened by either daylight or moonshine. It consists of special photos of Mom, laced with her favorite scarves, jewelry, and small meaningful art objects, including new things I occasionally buy for her. Yes, as crazy as it might sound, I still buy her things, which is, itself, a ritual. It started shortly after she passed away, when I saw a necklace she would have loved. As I stared at it, riding one of those emotional waves, my friend who was with me said, "It's never too late to accessorize!" It was freeing to follow my heart's desire to get it for her and place it on the altar.

As part of my ritual, I light candles for my mother and place light pink roses on her altar. Here, I write to her, talk to her, sing to her, and simply spend time with her. Another way that helps me to feel Mom's presence is to engage in things that she loved doing: walking in the rain, eating raspberries, or indulging in an ice cream sundae. I talk to her when I gaze at the moon. I intentionally wear her ring, spray her favorite perfume on my heart, listen to her favorite music, and dance with her spirit. I even got my first tattoo in honor of her and our endless love.

Ritual offers a way to ground you when you feel lost. It is an avenue to commune with your heart and the relationship with your beloved. It offers a therapeutic avenue to be with grief and also to be in communion with your loved one in a ways that transcends grief.

As you first begin to contemplate the possibilities for a ritual, ask yourself questions like: How does my heart want to express my love for my loved one? What brings honor to my beloved? What demonstrates my love so that I can feel the love and connection now? If my beloved were right here, what would I express? How can I go deeper into our connection – how can I taste it, feel it, touch it, see it and pour into it? What is aching to be expressed? How does the connection want to be known now?

Allow images to float into your conscious mind that give direction and form to your ritual and the sacred objects that want to be part of it.

Give permission for the ritual to unfold in some unexpected ways.

28
MEDITATION PRACTICE

Some of the most powerful personal growth happens in times of great challenge. As you live through difficult times, you find that this is exactly what takes place – amazingly, somehow, you *live* through it. And as you live through it, you may gain insight into a core part of yourself that stays intact, even when the rest of you might be a mess.

This core aspect of your self is the focus in meditation. By sitting with yourself, usually with eyes closed, you are giving yourself a "time-out" of the busyness of life. Meditation time is dedicated to dwelling within, rather than focusing on external factors or on the distracting mental gymnastics. Instead of fueling the usual obsessive thoughts you have about your life, you re-direct your attention to the practice of witnessing. Meditation is the practice of observing sensations, thoughts, feelings, and breath... as it all comes and goes.

There is an ineffable and mysterious aspect of you that stays intact, throughout everything. It is referred to by many names: the Witnesser, the Bigger Self, Essence, Soul, Spirit, Emptiness, Purity, Space, True Self, Inner Self, God, Love, The Higher Self, Light, Goddess, The Great Spirit, the Core Self – and these are just some of the ways of naming it.

Meditation practice strengthens your awareness of the Witnesser – the observer inside of you that witnesses what you are experiencing. The key in any difficult time is to learn how to anchor into this Witnesser. By practicing witnessing, one begins to identify less with life circumstances and becomes more aware of this core aspect of Self.

Meditation practice can be the surfboard through the ocean waves of emotion and mental agitation.

As you meditate, you learn to sit with the grief. This strengthens and anchors you into your core. Said in another way, meditation practice can help you to contact inner resources that did *not* get stripped away by your loss and devastation.

The reason why it is called "practice" is because this is exactly what it is. You sit. You practice witnessing. The practice is more important than the result. You may or may not feel quiet inside. You may or may not feel any sense of this Core Self. Allow expectations to fall away, along with everything else. The point is to witness *all* that arises and subsides...

One meditation approach is to imagine your self as the vast sky. All thoughts, images, feelings, and sensations are cloud formations that emerge, transform moment by moment, and dissolve. Your core self is the spaciousness. The clouds come and go. This is the practice. You just sit and welcome each sensation, feeling, thought. Instead of getting entangled in the web of thoughts and feelings, allow them to float through you... Be sky. This is the practice of sitting and watching the mind.

Rumi, a 13th-century Persian poet, scholar, and Sufi mystic, expressed this beautifully in his poem called "The Guest House":

This being human is a guest house.
Every morning a new arrival.

A joy, a depression, a meanness,
some momentary awareness comes
as an unexpected visitor.

Welcome and entertain them all!
Even if they're a crowd of sorrows,
who violently sweep your house
empty of its furniture,
still, treat each guest honorably.
He may be clearing you out
for some new delight.

The dark thought, the shame, the malice,
meet them at the door laughing, and invite them in.

Be grateful for whoever comes,
because each has been sent
as a guide from beyond.

Meditation practice softens the inclination to judge and opens the doorway into compassion.

29
THE POWER OF MANTRA

The word "mantra" is defined as a sound vibration that arises from the purest state of consciousness, and it is said to have the power to bring you back to this state. It can serve as a life preserve that keeps your head above the ocean waves of the mind. Repetition of the mantra, called *japa* in Sanskrit, is a great way to practice meditation.

For over twenty years, I have received the great company of the Sanskrit mantra, *Om Namah Shivaya*. This mantra has become my companion, my refuge, my strength, my friend, my protection, and my equanimity. It is a mantra that is known throughout the world. People from all different nationalities and languages repeat this mantra.

Om Namah Shivaya loosely translates to mean: "I bow to the light/God that is within me." *Om* is the primordial sound vibration of the Universe. *Namah* translates to mean "the Name" – naming the pure. *Shivaya* refers to the Divine.

I recommend the practice of a sound mantra because the mind is inclined to think, and then think about the thinking, and then, think some more. Simply, the mind likes to think. This is just what the mind does. It is rarely quiet. Repeating the mantra gives the mind something healthy to chew on. All you do is repeat the mantra over and over. Sanskrit is known as a sacred language. It is the liturgical language of Hinduism, Buddhism, and Jainism. The name *Sanskrit* means "refined," "consecrated," and "sanctified." It has always been regarded as the "high" language and used mainly for religious and scientific discourse. I believe it has the power to shift the biochemistry of the brain with its pure sound vibrations. I also prefer the use of Sanskrit because the mind cannot debate it as it could with affirmations. If you think to yourself, "I am at peace," then your mind can argue with itself and say, "No I'm not!" Using Sanskrit bypasses the possibility of debate.

Mantra repetition has the power to quiet the mind. If you find yourself getting distracted with other thoughts and not able to stay focused on the mantra, practice repeating the mantra out loud. You will probably discover that it is very difficult to get wrapped up in other thoughts while you are repeating the mantra out loud.

The use of *Om Namah Shivaya* is not religious or connected to a doctrine. You do not have to belong to a spiritual path to repeat it. It is universal and all-inclusive.

Repeating the mantra can invoke a sense of powerful presence. Your mind does not have to understand the mantra or even like it. All you need to do is repeat it and discover for yourself how it serves you. It does not reduce the grief but it can be used as a way of finding your center during times of turbulence.

Let's practice japa. With the inhale, Om Namah Shivaya. With the exhale, Om Namah Shivaya. Another approach is to repeat Om with your inhale, and Namah Shivaya with your exhale.

Again and again, with each breath, the mantra, *Om Namah Shivaya...*

Drop deeper and deeper inside of yourself. *Om Namah Shivaya, Om Namah Shivaya...*

Witness, breathe, and give yourself to the mantra.

It can only help.

30
INTENTIONALLY CHANGE
THE GRIEF CHANNEL

There comes a time when the weariness and sorrow of "the grief channel" is just too much and you must take a break. The enormity of grief triggers the fight-or-flight response, which leads to physical, mental, emotional exhaustion. You aren't designed to endure being in the *intensity* of grief *all* the time.

For many people, "the grief channel" changes on its own. But for others, it does not, which leads to the necessity to intentionally change the grief channel to something else.

To shift from "the grief channel," literally visualize changing the channel. Think of a television. When you pick up the remote and change the channel, you know that the channel you are leaving is still accessible, but you are simply choosing to tune into another channel. It is the same with grief. When you change the channel, it doesn't make grief disappear. It is not about denying grief. It's still there, but your focus is on another channel.

Grief changes with the passage of time. There comes a time when you will probably feel the desire to change the channel. No one can tell you when that time is. The timing for this shift organically arises from your own knowingness and guidance.

31
DIFFERENTIATE BETWEEN
HEALTHY AND UNHEALTHY GRIEF

It is important to distinguish between healthy grieving and an experience of grief that is unhealthy. Grief, by nature, is a roller costar ride of emotion. Crying, being mad, feeling lost, feeling numb, not wanting to socialize, feeling needy, needing to take time off from work, being moody, acting bratty, feeling like a zombie are all part of the ride. Statements like "I don't want to be here without him" or "I will never be able to get past this" are not uncommon in the grieving process. Heartache can feel like the heart is breaking, like shattered glass splintering each moment of breath. It can feel almost intolerable, "getting through it" moment to moment, hour by hour. This is often all part of a healthy, natural grieving process.

However, if there is no break from unbearable pain, if you are having suicidal fantasies, if you are incapacitated, if you are isolating and avoiding contact with others, I think it is fair to say that you may be stuck in an unhealthy grieving process. This might also manifest in other symptoms, such as addictive behaviors and self-destructive patterns. Whether it is alcohol, drugs, pain medicines or sleeping pills, isolation, sexual obsession, overeating, under-eating, bulimia, anorexia, disappearing into the TV, obsessive surfing the web, excessive exercise, rushing, busyness, porn, never sleeping, always sleeping... bottom line, you are hurting yourself. Addictive behaviors are attempts to get away from the pain, but they only make it worse. Self-destructive behaviors may look like they are temporally helping but they will inevitably make more of a mess in your life. And, besides, the grief only waits for you, ready to move in with an intensity – once you stop the self-abuse. After all that avoidance, you find out that it never left.

If you are involved in self-destructive behaviors, recognize it as grief on a loud speaker screaming out for help.

Unhealthy grieving can also manifest as resistance to spending time with the grief. This often leads to feeling immobilized, ungrounded and foggy – and you may be so "out of it" that you might not even associate your experience with the grief.

As already stated, trauma of loss can trigger Post Traumatic Stress

Disorder, or PTSD, which brings about acute changes in the biochemistry and hormones, gearing the body up for reaction and survival. Faced with the stressor, in this case grief, PTSD mobilizes the body to fight, flee, or freeze. The unconscious mind believes that you are in danger and that you must gear up into these survival modes. Fight, flight, or freeze mechanisms were designed for urgent times of danger, not to be sustained over time. If not interrupted, some sort of collapse is inevitable.

Thus, it may not be possible to intentionally change "the grief channel" on your own. This is not something to be embarrassed about. Grief is one of the biggest challenges in living life and one of the most important times to reach out for more support.

32
SEEKING PROFESSIONAL HELP

The wisdom to know when to ask for extra support is a strength, not a weakness. Seeking support rises from the desire to care for your self. It is in the action of asking for help that demonstrates your commitment to yourself. You are taking a stand to not allow more loss – the loss of yourself.

The trauma of loss is indeed a time to ask for help, to learn to lean on others and to allow your needs to be known. Pursuing professional guidance is a gift to yourself and can offer you necessary support.

It is also a time to allow your self to be in connection with others who are also suffering with loss. This is why bereavement support groups are so popular. They meet the genuine deep need to be in the company of other people who are experiencing similar feelings and issues.

Seeking professional help is not a weakness or a failure in any way. Remember, grief has a life of its own. It is not the grief itself that is the problem. Grief is not an obstruction that needs to go away. Professional help offers ways to broaden your sense of resourcefulness so that you can deal with the trauma. Speaking with a professional is different than talking with a friend. In seeking help, you will have a guide who understands PTSD, loss and grief. Through this therapeutic relationship and guidance, you will learn to effectively respond to yourself with more acceptance, compassion and tools.

33
WHEN YOU FIRST MET DEATH

By gaining insight into what your first experiences were with death and loss, as well as your family's reactions, can deepen your sense of understanding and compassion for how you are approaching your current loss.

My first exposure to "death" that I can remember was when I was three and my goldfish died. It was the same day that my grandma died. I didn't quite understand what it meant that grandma was gone but I cried and cried for the loss of my fish. All I knew was that I had loved watching and feeding my goldfish every day; she swam around the tank, gold, slippery, shining and beautiful. And then on this day for some reason she was lying on her side and not moving at all. NOT AT ALL! My mom explained that she had died. I was sobbing. Why, why would she just die? My mom was also crying – for the loss of her mother-in-law. When I got a little older, Mom told me that she had wondered if I was grieving Grandma that day and didn't know it. But all I remember was screaming, "My fish! My fish!" I was obsessed. And I didn't fall for the line that we would get another fish. I knew a new fish could not replace my fish that I loved, and a new fish wouldn't make my sweet friend come back.

Two years later, when I was five, I was playing in front of my house and I witnessed a little kitten running down the side of the street and fall into a hole that adults referred to as a sewer. I ran to the sewage hole to try to save this precious little white kitty but to no avail. And so at the age of five, I was horrified by how bad things could happen to innocent creatures.

What was your first meeting with impermanence? I invite you to take a moment and write down your reflections. What was your first experience of "death?" What were your responses? How did your family respond? What beliefs did you internalize about death and loss? How does this impact how you are responding today to your loss?

Can you imagine a first-time exposure to death that would naturally lead to a more positive approach to your loss today? Pause for a moment and think about it. Write down this imagined experience and then write down the newly created beliefs that emerge from it. Once you write them down, read them to yourself, out loud. Now, imagine that these beliefs about death and loss are part of your foundation.

It is an interesting process to re-write your own history – to even contemplate what you would have wanted for yourself, and to find a way to give it to yourself in the present through envisioning it and feeling into it. It has been found that when you think about an experience and visualize it happening, the same physiological state is triggered as if it is actually occurring. So, although you can't literally change your history, you can re-write your script, change your beliefs, and affect how you approach your life and how you respond to losses.

34
KEEP BREATHING AND
KEEP HOLDING HANDS

Navigating through grief can simply mean that you keep on breathing and you hold someone's hand. Sometimes this is the only thing you can do... just breathe... feel whatever arises... and hold on tight to a person's hand who loves you and with whom you feel safe.

Breathe. Hold hands. Feel the warmth of the hand holding yours.

Practice bringing your attention to the comfort of this warm hand holding yours and allow it to serve as a kinesthetic mantra - a way to focus your mind and anchor a sense of grounding and comfort.

Breathe and focus on your hand being held. Again and again...

Just hold on.

And be held.

Feel... Breathe... Hold on...

Yes, keep breathing... and keep holding hands...

This takes you through.

35

THE FORGIVENESS PROCESS

The forgiveness process is ongoing. It begins the moment you know of your loss. Every feeling you experience, from anger to despair, from abandonment to sorrow, from guilt to emptiness, is part of the forgiveness process.

A tremendous sense of separation often accompanies loss – separation from the one you grieve, from God, from yourself, and often from people who are in our lives. When loss occurs, people often enter into a spiritual crisis and ask questions like "Why did this happen to me?" "How could God let this happen?" or "Why would the Universe unfold this?" A sense of hopelessness and despair is often directed towards God – blaming God for not protecting or healing the loved one. Anger is also often directed at oneself – for something you didn't do, or for something you did do that you now regret. The mind is inclined to blame someone, something, God, ourselves, anyone! It fights with reality, making "it" wrong.

Often there is a necessary forgiveness process with the one who has departed that weighs heavy on the heart. Unfinished issues, unfulfilled needs, hurtful exchanges that still sting. All the communications that didn't take place yet. The issues that we intended to work out sometime in the future. Sometimes new information comes to the surface after the loved one passes that triggers major upset. One of my bereaved clients discovered that her partner was a gambler and he left her a financial mess to clean up. Another client was reading through his spouse's diaries and discovered that she was having an affair. No one likes being left with unresolved issues. But it happens because in general, people tend to delay talking about challenging issues and people are inclined to be conflict-avoidant. Unfortunately, procrastination can be one of the biggest regrets when it becomes too late.

Often loss also triggers unexpected interpersonal dynamics between family members and friends. Unfinished issues that were patched over can resurface with a vengeance, furthering the hurt and sense of loss. The trauma of loss can bring out the worst, including controlling tendencies and irrational, reactive patterns of relating.

The good news is that for most issues, there is a way to grow into forgiveness. But it can't be rushed.

As a psychotherapist, I am often asked, "How do I forgive?" First, I will tell you what absolutely doesn't work – and that is pretending that there is nothing to forgive!

Instead, give permission to feel your feelings, especially the ones you don't want to feel. This means moving through the anger – allowing it and expressing it in safe ways – as part of the forgiveness process. Often people feel strange about expressing anger at someone who is "dead," but remember, the relationship does not die with your beloved.

You can address the unresolved issues directly by writing letters to your deceased beloved or by talking about them with a professional. People often don't understand that expressing anger is in the direction towards forgiveness. You can't skip steps. Forgiveness is often a process, not just a decision.

Often people think that forgiveness means to move on and try not to be angry. But actually, being real with the anger and other feelings is like peeling an onion – through the tears and anger, you eventually come into genuine forgiveness. Acceptance and forgiveness are intrinsically interwoven. We can't *make* forgiveness or acceptance happen; they both have elements of grace to them. So, expressing anger *with the intention to grow into forgiveness* is part of the path of healing.

Be aware of what your authentic truth is and allow it. Trust in the process. The process of forgiving calls for surrendering into what you feel. Surrendering often brings forth a sense of an internal "burning." As you feel the intensity of the feelings, it may feel like you are on fire – and the alchemy of fire changes you. There is nothing you can do but burn through the resistance, the tears and the staggering pain. This is the surrendering.

In time, the gifts or lessons of why something unfolded in your life may be revealed. You may see changes in yourself that you value. Because of your loss, you may grow to be stronger, more compassionate, resilient, aware and grateful.

Maya Angelou, an acclaimed American author, poet, dancer, actress, and singer, sheds light on how to forgive:

You may not control all the events that happen to you, but you can decide not to be reduced by them ...You can't forgive without loving. And I don't mean sentimentality. I don't mean mush. I mean having enough courage to stand up and say, "I forgive. I'm finished with it."

Sometimes it can take time – a very long time – to be able to say, "I'm done with this. It is history." The fact that it takes a long time, in and of itself, calls for forgiveness.

All in time, forgiveness happens.

Or not. And if that is the case, that is also to be forgiven.

36
THE CHALLENGES TO
RECEIVING SUPPORT

When loss occurs, often there is an outpouring of support. Mourners have shared with me that they don't know how to actually take in and receive the abundance of the love and support coming their way. They tell me that they don't know what to do with it. If this is true for you, experiment with visualizing a place of "receiving" in your heart that you can take in the love and support. Allow yourself to truly see an image of your "receiving spot." Know what it looks like in detail. Examples have been described as: an open beautiful vase, a perfectly formed bird's nest, a huge hand-made woven basket, a flourishing flower garden, a tranquil lake, a shipping dock that receives the delivery of love packages.

Another challenge when it comes to receiving support is how difficult it is to find words to express the gratitude that arises at such a raw time. Saying "thank you" doesn't seem like enough. Support is tremendously appreciated but the resources to express the gratitude may be minimal. If this is how you feel, just know that no one is expecting anything from you. Contrary to what you may think, "thank you" *is* enough!

Many bereaved clients also share that as much as they appreciate the many offers to join people in this or that, they don't want to do a lot of things or be with a lot of people. It can feel paradoxical to lean into receiving and yet not overextend in order to placate other people's desires to be helpful. Saying no to others, and possibly disappointing them, might not have been a strength before the loss and now it might feel even harder – but it's essential. Bottom line, you are going to receive a lot of offers to have company and do things, and you are *not* going to want to do all those things.

This time is about *you;* this you must remember. Everyone who is supporting you wants what is best for you, which must ultimately be determined by you. You aren't expected to "get it right." You learn as you go. If you become isolated and depressed, you may be overdoing it with declining offers. If you become exhausted, you may be staying too busy and socializing too much and avoiding time with yourself.

Being showered with love and support can trigger worthiness issues that you may have thought were handled a long time ago. In response you might feel a sense of discomfort and awkwardness. At a time when you don't even recognize yourself in many ways, and you certainly are not enjoying yourself, it may feel ironic to be surrounded by people who want to spend time with you, sharing how it is a privilege to be with you and support you. What do you do with that?

And what do you do with the experience that although so many people love you and are around you, you *still feel* so alone, in pain, and so empty?

You breathe. You surrender. You feel whatever you feel. You receive to whatever degree you can receive. You let your ego be uncomfortable. You let the emptiness be there. You allow people to reach out to you, whether you feel alone or not. Let the love do its medicinal thing that it organically does. You don't have to control it. You *can't* control it. Believe people when they are telling you that they really want to be there for you. Breathe again. Inhale, exhale. This is all you can do.

Sometimes the experience of support is the opposite, and the people you think will show up for you, don't. The result is tremendous disappointment that is intensified because it is such a raw and emotional time. Sometimes people will tell me that through this time of loss, they realize that they don't really have a strong support system. How painful is that? Or, you may find that support floods in during the first few months after the loss and then life goes on as usual — for others.

If your support system is not what you need it to be, I strongly encourage you to create more support. This is not a time to go without! Tell people in your life what you need. And, attend bereavement groups to be with other fellow club members, who are also seeking support.

We need others in this journey, even though it doesn't take away the pain. You are not meant to do this alone, even if you feel alone.

37
THE POWER OF WORDS

There is great power to words. They color the lens through which we perceive through and thus, how we experience life. They provoke images, sensations, feelings and meanings.

Contemplate what words you use to describe the loss of your beloved.

The words listed below have different connotations and meanings. People are inclined to use certain words more than others, depending on family background, religious conditioning, personal spiritual inclinations, beliefs and values.

Notice what images, feelings and sensations arise for you as you slowly read the following words and phrases:

Died
Dead
Passed Away
Gone
Completed
Disembodied
Deceased
Departed
Buried
Left
Delivered
Transitioned
Returned
Homecoming
Plucked

Which words resonate most with you in regard to your loss?
Which words are you least comfortable with?
Which words are you drawn to use more often?

In my grieving process, it has been important for me to visit with all of these words. I found that when I announced out loud that my mom "died" and is "gone," it brought home the horrible finality that

I had to face. When using the words "returned," "transitioned," or "departed," I could feel an opening to the possibility of connecting with Mom's spirit and the presence of the mystery.

All of these words have a place. Yet, how would the relationship to mortality be different if we, as children, were raised with words like "returned," "transitioned," or "homecoming" instead of "dead," "deceased," and "gone"?

As a process of self-exploration, you may want to experiment with the various terminologies and be aware of the impact your language has on your experience.

38
HONORING THE
HEART'S WISDOM

In grief, a visceral experience of the heart is unavoidable.

Listening to the heart with tenderness, acceptance, and compassion deepens trust in oneself and gives a glimmer of hope for restoration.

The heart speaks through the language of your body's sensations.

Feelings arise, sensations come and go, all of which are out of the ego's control.

The journey of the heart calls for surrender and respect.

Grief is a dark and foggy time, a journey into unknown territory. Yet, it can also be a time of crystal clarity about what actually touches and moves the heart and what doesn't. In response to grief from others, empathy can truly move the heart, while polite gestures often slide right off the skin. The heart just knows. The heart is wise.

Great sages have been known to say that the heart is the abode of the divine; tears are the sweat of the heart; and the stirrings of the heart tell you what is real.

The heart is resilient. It naturally goes towards healing, just like the face of the sunflower follows the sun's rays. Similar to the physical body, the emotional heart is inclined to heal itself, if given the opportunity to do so.

39
FOR THOSE SUPPORTING
THE BEREAVED

Despite good intentions, statements like "She had a long life" or "He had a great life" or "It will get better in time" do not help to console the bereaved in the way you hope for them to. These sayings often fall empty. Telling someone that "It's alright" is one of those examples – because it truly does not *feel* okay – unless the person who died was suffering so badly. But even then, it might not feel okay. It is important to not assume anything.

Approach the bereaved with humbleness and an inner posture that you do not know the depth of their grieving process, what he or she may be feeling or how they should "get through" it. It is important not to judge grief or even attempt to give guidance unless asked for it. Instead, understand that grief has its own way and is unique for each person.

A little more advice for the person in the support role: Don't bother trying to make your bereaved friend or family member feel better. It is not a time to feel better.

Just be compassionate. Be tender. Take your person's hand and genuinely validate their pain with heartfelt empathy. The person grieving is extra sensitive to vibration. Bring your heart, that's it. You don't have to *do* anything. Just let them know that you know that it sucks and that you are there *with* them. Be a gentle presence and a safe space for whatever feelings arise. If you are comfortable with touch, you can offer to hold him or her. If are uncomfortable with touch, or you don't feel touch is appropriate, you can offer to wrap her or him with a blanket or shawl, to give a sense of containment, comfort and safety.

Remember that the person grieving may be moody, over-reactive, sensitive, emotional, and can get overwhelmed easily. You can do him or her a great favor and not take any of it personally. And when he or she apologizes, you can accept the apology and say, "You have a right to feel cruddy and to be moody."

If your attempts to support your friend or family member appear to be ineffective, remember that it is not your fault. It's not about you. Remember, you can bypass all guessing games and directly ask, "How can I best support you?" This question communicates respect and deep caring.

Even though you can't take away the pain, your steady and loving presence absolutely makes a difference and speaks volumes to a person in grief. How people show up during the grief process has a lasting effect.

It is essential to take care of yourself so that you do not drown in the grief with them. By taking care of yourself, you will have the resources to sustain being there through time. Sometimes the support person will ask me, "Is it okay if I laugh in front of them? I feel guilty for having fun. What should I do?" What is most important is that you are yourself. If you have lightness in your heart, bring it. If you are sad, bring it. Sometimes your lightness can help your person to laugh. The distractions of laughter and fun are not insults to grief. They do not take away from grieving. Comic relief is good medicine. The great singer/songwriter Joni Mitchell refers to laughing and crying as the same release.

It is up to the bereaved to tell you if something you are doing is too much. Don't make these decisions for them. Bring respect to the grieving process and remember it shows itself in unexpected, non-linear ways.

I want to walk with you through this time. We will walk slowly. We will stop whenever you need to; I will be with you as you feel what you need to, and then we'll keep going. – Anonymous

Rearranged, Never the Same: The Nature of Grief

THE SILVER LINING

40
IS THERE A SILVER LINING, PLEASE?

The good news is that the fact that you hurt this much means that you also love this much. There is no way to avoid this level of grief unless you locked yourself into a room and never loved again. But of course that would only usher in another kind of grief – the grief of endless missed opportunities to love.

In the worst times of grief, I have heard many people ask, "Is it worth it? Is it worth loving someone so much that it hurts this badly?"

I believe the answer is, "Yes, oh yes, it is."

Beauty shows itself even in the deepest pain. Marilyn Sewell expresses this sentiment perfectly.

If we live long enough in this world, we will have our hearts broken. Do they heal? Well, maybe not fully, completely ever. But in the cracked and broken pieces, that's where the light shines through.

Would you trade the light to have your beloved back again?

Yes.

But that's not how it works.

In time, as life goes one, the light usually does shine through again.

It might not be very bright for a while but it is there...

It comes through many channels – from the love and support of others, the innocence of a purring cat curled up on your lap, your dog's excitement to see you walk through your doorway, or a child's shameless giggles. Life keeps happening and so does the love.

41
WHOLE INCLUDES THE HOLE

Once loss occurs, it is woven into the fabric of your being. It is not something that you "overcome," like an obstacle. It is not something you work through, as one does with personal growth issues. It is an inherent part of living.

My experience is that the loss of someone that I love leaves a hole. After living with this hole for years, allowing it to be there, and growing to recognize that it doesn't go away, an organic re-organizing occurs. There is a surrendering and an embracing. Life grows back, through and around the hole, just like ivy vines wind their way through an opening in the bark of a tree.

In time, I have grown to accept that the hole is part of who I am. The word "wholeness" communicates something different to me than it did before. For the first time I saw how the word "whole" includes the word "hole" in it.

The hole is part of the whole.

It can be freeing to know that you don't have to get rid of the hole in order to feel whole again.

42
MOVING TOWARDS
BEING PRESENT

The recovery process with grief ultimately moves one towards living as fully in the present moment as possible. With each loss, our own mortality feels closer and becomes more real. As we face impermanence, the silver lining is in the passionate desire to live fully and be fiercely alive.

No matter what arises – from the horrible to the beautiful – it is all life itself and to be lived thoroughly. The more you show up with all of yourself to whatever it is, the more alive you feel. This awareness, commitment, and conviction can shift depression into a sense of awakening. There is a choice – you either resist what you are feeling or you go with it, embrace it and soften.

A great practice for inviting yourself more into the present moment is to drop out of your head and into your body. By noticing the sensations in your body, you are no longer locked into the circles of your self-talk, but rather you are paying attention to the experience you are presently having in your skin. Feel the sensations in your body without trying to explain them to yourself. For example, your self-talk might typically say: "This tightness in my stomach is from that talk that I had with Debbie about the funeral. I knew I shouldn't have..." Stop! Instead, just notice the tightness in your stomach and breathe into it. Allow. Stay focused on the sensations. You might be aware of where you feel warm or cold, tight or loose, fluid or contracted. The self-talk can now shift to a witnessing voice and goes more like this: "I notice the tightness in my stomach. It feels like a fist in my tummy. It is hard and tight. I can hardly breathe. I notice that this tightness radiates up into my throat, which is also tight and shut down. As I am noticing this, the fist in my tummy softens a bit and I am now aware of my breath, deepening and allowing my shoulders to drop. " And here you are – in the present moment.

Another practice is to intensify your experience of your senses. The senses offer an excellent way to ground into the now. They are portals into the present moment. Experiment with this. First, intensify your awareness into your ability to see. Notice what is before you – the colors, textures, and shapes... Just notice and *see* everything with crystal clarity and definition. Practice right now. Truly, this very moment. Breathe and notice what it is like to truly see. How does this impact your sense of being in this present moment?

Now, experiment with your ability to hear. Intensify your awareness of the sounds you are hearing, right now. Notice. This can include the sound of your breath or of quietness. Just notice the sounds. Amplify them. Turn the volume up on the gift of hearing sounds. What do you notice happens as you tune into the many sounds of *this* here and now?

Now, shift your awareness to your nose, the vehicle for your olfactory sense. It is said that this sense opens your brain to memory like nothing else. Give yourself something yummy to smell and be present to the scent. Ahhhh... Scents have the power to transport you and shift your nervous system.

Now, turn your attention to touch. The kinesthetic sense is a powerful portal for deepening into the present moment. Tune into your body. What part of your body is calling out for healing touch? Bring your palms of your hands to this part of your body and feel into the sensations of your own touch. We all have great healing power in our own hands that is often underutilized. Breathe into your touch. Allow your body to soak in the healing tidings.

Now, shift your hands so that one palm lies on your belly, right under your belly button and your other hand rests on your heart, the center of your chest on your breastbone. This is a healing holding posture. Try it on. Notice. Slow down enough to pay attention and be in the present moment. This is a great posture for grounding yourself and bringing a sense of protection and safety.

Experiment with touching someone else, or touching a soft object, or allowing yourself to be touched. Notice what it is like to bring all of your attention to what it feels like to touch and be touched. You can even bring your awareness to the sensation of your clothes on your skin. The kinesthetic sense is an excellent portal into experiencing the present moment.

And, it is the same with taste. Mindfully eat or drink something yummy, paying close attention to the sensations of taste, how the food or drink feels in your mouth as you take it in, as you chew, as you swallow, as it goes down, through your throat into your stomach. Go for it – put something delicious into your mouth, close your eyes, and truly experience the portal of taste. *Bam*, you disappear into the present moment.

This is it: the present moment. It doesn't mean you aren't having hard feelings. It just means that even during the grief process, only the present exists.

43
IS IT OKAY FOR ME
TO ENJOY MY LIFE AGAIN?

Many people in the grieving process feel guilty when they find themselves enjoying their lives again. They ask me, "Does this mean I'm not grieving anymore? Is that okay? Do I still love them if I am not grieving as much as I was? Is this okay?"

The answer is an unequivocal yes! It is okay! And it is no reflection on your love.

Even though it may be hard to believe, you may experience a stronger sense of connection with your beloved as you enjoy your life again, rather than in grief. All in time.

Sometimes people report that more grief arises when they start opening to enjoyment. "When I find myself enjoying life, I miss her even more because I just want to share it with her." Some people who have lost their spouses often wonder if opening to loving another equates betrayal of some sort.

The truth is that grieving doesn't stop when enjoyment re-enters one's life or even when a new love interest happens. The presence of enjoyment or even new companionship does not replace the one who has departed.

In the nature of grief, permission must be given to all feelings, and this includes good feelings too. Part of the grieving process is "coming back to life," meaning emerging and returning to a sense of well-being, feeling enlivened and excited to live again. Similarly to how spring inevitably follows winter, so is the natural process of healing.

There can be cultural influences on the timing for when it is okay to live and enjoy life again after a loss. In Crete and some parts of Greece, widows and mothers will continue to mourn and wear only black for the rest of their lives. In some cultures, one is supposed to mourn for forty days before re-entering normal life. Even in the United States there may be gossip about a woman re-marrying in less than a year's time after the death of her husband.

One of my clients described her grieving process as "needing to go into a cave." And then, when she felt it was time to come out of the cave and "live again," she was unsure if it was okay. But she knew it was time.

Everyone has his or her own way. Why judge any of it? Some people find new partners quickly. It doesn't mean that they didn't love the person who died or that they are not grieving.

Always give yourself to the enjoyment of life when it comes your way. It is a gift and not to be missed. Enjoyment can offer you an opportunity to feel your beloved through another avenue besides grief. Enjoyment opens the door to transcending the sense of separation.

44

THE UNITY IN GRIEF

In the book *The Soul in Grief*, Robert Romanyshyn writes beautifully about how grief and reverie for life unfold into one another and intermingle. In speaking about his opening to reverie through grieving his wife of twenty-five years, he says:

It felt to me that I had a direct experience of the wheel of life and death, which encompasses all creation. ...Grief's heart yearns for reverie and its moments of reprieve. For the soul in grief, reverie is a balm, which soothes the pain, the brief moment of respite when all is still, when the world and its demands are briefly silenced ...In reverie everyday, ordinary things, things as simple as dust, become a blank page, inviting a new start. In reverie I was standing on that shore where the tides of grief were eroding the ground beneath my feet. But for a moment it was the sounds of the tides of grief which mattered. These sounds comforted my tired soul.

There is a sense of unity with everything in how all that is born inevitably dies and all who love inevitably grieve. In the very darkest moments of grief is the poignant connection with all of life. Inherent in the depths of loss is an awareness of the oneness with every species, every sentient being, and how we are all spinning in this cycle of life and death together.

Death and grief transcend borders of countries and differences in politics, races, cultures, and species. There is documentation of how many other species grieve for their loved ones – it is not just a human phenomena.

In nearly all species of monkey, the bereaved mother will carry her child's lifeless body around with her for days, holding the limp body close to her, showing great signs of sorrow. It has been observed and documented that when the leader of a troop of toque macaques is killed, the others gather in silence around his body. Even his old rivals show their deference, tenderly touching their fallen leader.

Elephants form strong bonds with the others in the herd and when one dies, the rest of the herd mourns. When a baby dies, the mother stays at the site of departure for days, often not leaving until there are signs of danger. Mothers and aunts alike mourn the calf, with eyes sunken and ears drooping, visibly sullen and somber. They often return again and again to the location site of where the death took place. The herd takes great care in the burial of the dead. The elephants walk to and fro in search of leaves and twigs that they use to cover the body of the deceased.

A small band of elephants was observed during a drought that scorched the already parched African plain, drying up the tiny waterholes. The youngest lagged behind and finally stopped. For two days, as he grew weaker from thirst, his mother stood over him, shading him from the sun. When the youngster eventually died, his mother tried to pull him up with her trunk. Mourning her loss, she hung her head low and moaned, with tears flowing from her eyes.

There is a famous story of a caregiver and rescuer of elephants in Africa who died in his house. Shortly after, lines of elephants were seen walking from all directions out of the jungle and circled his house, showing their grief and respect.

With dolphins, when a baby is born, the mother has to lead it to the surface of the ocean for it to breathe. Even if a baby dolphin is dead, a mother will still do this and will hold it for a very long time, maybe even hours, until she finally accepts the death and lets the baby dolphin go.

Grief is a doorway into realizing our unity with all species within this web of life and death. Grief opens us to reverence for all of life. Hopefully this is something we will never forget.

45
"BACK TO LIFE"

When you are going through hell, keep going.
— Anonymous

"Back to life" does not mean that when grieving, you are not living life. Rather, it refers to the process of embracing life as it is. Being alive with all of it – the heartache, the sweetness, the joy, the warmth, the devastation, the tenderness, the fullness, and the emptiness.

"Back to life" refers to the continuation of life that happens even after huge loss.

"Back to life" is the ability to open to new experiences and to allow them to become part of the makings of your new life.

As one tunnels through the grief canal and starts to see an opening, there is a surrendering, an acceptance, and an invitation to enjoy life again.

In your deepest self, you probably know that your beloved wants you to enjoy life again and if they could talk to you, this would be their exact advice and encouragement.

Life shows us how vast we truly are in experiencing many different emotions. We can grieve as we can also be in love with a new person, or be joyful with the birth of a new grand baby or feel passionate about starting a new career.

Grief is a wild ride – first you need to learn to give yourself permission to feel the sorrow, and then, at some point, it is time to give yourself permission to experience joy again.

Rearranged, Never the Same: The Nature of Grief

TWO HANDS –
One Hand, Grief;
One Hand, Connection

46
TWO HANDS

On one hand, there is the grief that keeps on grieving. This hand represents the loss, the impact of the absence of the beloved, and all the feelings and issues that accompany the grieving process.

And the other hand holds the possibility of the continuation of relationship. This hand represents the awareness that love does not die. Forms change, but love remains strong, and the relationship with the beloved also does not die.

In my own grieving process, from the moment Mom left her body, I declared that more than anything, I wanted to maintain a "current relationship" with her. Beyond having memories, I felt drawn to a knowingness that I could have new experiences with her. This conviction, in and of itself, inspired a doorway to open and it is here that I saw a very clear image of two hands, both active: one hand, with palm facing downward with fingers curved inward representing the deep grieving process, and the other hand, palm facing up, representing openness to ongoing connection.

Humbling as it was, I found out that I couldn't *make* new experiences with my mom happen, no matter how much I wanted them to, no matter how I prepared myself, no matter how much I asked the Universe for them. Some people say the opposite. In fact, large numbers of books are written on how to make contact with those on the other side, utilizing many tools. I can't comment on these tools because I did not approach it in this way. I simply believed in the knowingness that the relationship continues and Mom is not only available but also desiring to be in contact. I believe that this inner posture of openness and *knowingness* that I am in an ongoing relationship was the key that allowed exactly that to happen.

Cookie, my college roommate's mother, helped me with this. It was in the mid-nineties when she transitioned and it was two weeks later that I received a message while I slept. I can't say for sure that it was from Cookie, but it was witty and direct, just like her. It was typed, letter-by-letter, word-by-word, into my third eye point, in the middle of my forehead:

You can't possibly know for sure, because you are there, but I am here and let me tell you something, it doesn't end there!

47
STAYING IN CURRENT RELATIONSHIP

I couldn't tell you what it meant when I first declared the words, "I want to stay in current relationship with Mom."

Upon Mom's passing, I felt deep longing to know Mom *now*, if only to glimpse into her present experience. I repeated the words over and over: *I am committed to stay in current relationship with Mom.* I didn't know how, but I was on fire with conviction that there is more than this dimension of existence and more than what is visible to the eye.

Through quantum physics, we've come to understand that the world as we see it is nothing more than what our brains allow us to see. If we do not have a picture in our minds of something, our brains do not acknowledge it and we cannot see it, even if it's right in front of us. In other words, if we do not have the conceptual blueprint for something, it is probably not going to be in our sense of reality. My conviction to being in current relationship with my mom became the blueprint for connection to take me through the rest of my life.

Each morning with meditation, I consciously invited my awareness to expand. I asked to develop my ability to know and see into the Mystery so that I could be in contact with Mom. I refused to buy into the illusion of death that implied she was gone forever and instead, dedicated my whole self to the desire to grow in relationship with her. I found myself paying close attention to everything possible that might be a communication. Just the process of entertaining the thought that she might communicate to me opened me up. Intently I gazed up into the vastness of the skies, the power of the trees, the aliveness of the birds, and the new spring green, and felt a sense of her rebirth. Seeking to drink of her continued presence, her beauty, her love, I stayed committed to the Universal principle, *Love Never Dies.*

Her favorite animal was the deer. On the day that Mom died at the hospital, my dad, sister, and I sadly made our way back home to my parent's house in the late evening. We were amazed to find ourselves greeted by a family of six deer in the driveway. This had never happened before. Likewise, on the day of her funeral, deer surrounded the house continually throughout the day – it was a most unusual occurrence, and we were all in awe.

Following the funeral, I waited for signs that this disappearing act of hers was not really as final as it appeared. She didn't respond to my requests as I had hoped. It was sobering and humbling to realize that I could not command contact to happen. It was not going to be on my time.

Instead, I thought about Cookie's message to me: *It doesn't end there.* I began to commune with Mom in my heart constantly – not through memories, but rather by talking with her, by feeling into her presence, and by opening – to allow for a glimpse into a connection that death could not take away.

48
WAYS OF OPENING
TO CONNECTION

Some people say that you have to have active faith and a strong desire in order for communication to take place. However, this is not always the case. Sometimes people who strongly believe do not experience connection, and sometimes people who don't believe unexpectedly have an experience.

My suggestion is to open yourself for contact, pay attention, and also know that it is not up to you to make it happen or not. Nor does it matter if you believe in it or not. It either happens or it doesn't. And, you may notice or you might not notice. Either way, experiment and be with the approach of "two hands."

Similar to any relationship and communication, you have to know you are in relationship and be open to communication. You can start the dialogue. You can listen for response. This deep listening opens you to the possibility of noticing messages that may occur through nature, music, dreams, media, books, spoken word, visions, writings, passing images, flickering lights, technology, inspiring thoughts and sometimes hearing your loved one's voice. The communication may be subtle or it may be obvious. The key is to pay attention. When the Mystery shows itself, there is a stirring within that cannot be denied or fabricated.

Some people utilize metaphysical tools and approaches to contact loved ones. Some of these techniques are mirror gazing, the Ouija Board, and the use of pendants to detect energies, as well as many other methods. I have not experimented with these techniques so I will not go into any detail about them. But I would feel remiss to not mention that there is a lot of information available on intentional ways to contact loved ones who are no longer embodied.

Most importantly, if you have not received a communication yet, stay out of the box of pessimism and fear. Communication comes when it comes. Be thankful for whatever you get. It may be a bit choppy and not a linear conversation. Refuse to fuel any doubts.

49
"NO BIRTH, NO DEATH"

Thich Nhat Hanh, the great Buddhist teacher, also experienced deep ongoing grief after his mother died, until he had a visit from her and he realized that she was not "gone."

In his book *No Death, No Fear*, Thich Nhat Hanh encourages us to look deeply to realize that there is no birth or death, but rather energy is always present and it moves in and out of being manifested as form. He states, "According to Buddha, to qualify something as existing or not existing is wrong. God transcends all notions, including the notions of creation and destruction, being and non-being." He compares the reality/non-reality to radio and television signals in a room in which the TV or radio isn't turned on. He says that of course the signals are there even if we don't have the TV or radio on. It is not correct to say they don't exist just because we aren't tuned into them at that moment.

He cautions us to not get so committed to our beliefs about death that we block ourselves from seeing outside of our perceptions. The focus of his writing is how nothing actually ever dies – it only changes form.

If you ask a cloud, "How old are you? What is the date of your birth? Before you were born, where were you?" you can listen deeply and you may hear a reply. You can imagine the cloud being born. Before being born, it was the water on the ocean's surface. Or it was in the river and then it became vapor. It was also the sun because the sun makes vapor. The wind is there too, helping the water to become a cloud. The cloud does not come from nothing; there has been only a change in form. It is not a birth of something out of nothing. Sooner or later, the cloud will change into rain or snow. If you look deeply into the rain, you can see the cloud. The cloud is not lost; it is transformed into rain, and the rain is transformed into grass and the grass into cows and then to milk and then into the ice cream you eat. Next time you eat ice cream, give yourself time to look at the ice cream and say: Hello cloud! I recognize you!

He goes on to explain:

Just as we can understand a cloud as a manifestation of something that has always been there, and rain as the end of the cloud manifestation, we can understand human beings and everything around us as a manifestation that has come from somewhere and will go nowhere. Manifestation is not the opposite of destruction. It simply changes form.

There is no "dead." Everything transforms. When candlelight is blown out, it transforms into smoke and vapor and joins the ether. Wood gives itself to fire and then ash, which recycles into earth. Everything is always becoming something else.

Baba Muktananda, the great Guru of Siddha Yoga who brought Siddha Yoga to the United States, also spoke about how death does not exist. He said that the subtle body, also known as the light body (the psycho-spiritual constituents of living beings) continues on after the physical body drops away, similarly to how a snake sheds its skin and manifests new skin. He emphasized that the physical body is nothing but a corpse at all times, imbued by the life energy of the subtle bodies. Baba described death as the withdrawal of the subtle energy bodies from the physical form, into other dimensions, leaving the corpse to be discarded in respectful ways, burial or cremation.

What changes for you in relation to "death" when you allow yourself to consider these teachings?

50
POP THE BALLOON

Yes, pop the balloon... and what happens? Does the air rise up to the heavens or does it merge with the air right here?

When you see a balloon, you probably don't wonder about the air inside of the balloon. You see the balloon's color, shape, and size – the personality, so to speak, of the balloon. But the balloon could not do what it was made to do without the air in the balloon. The air gives the balloon buoyancy and substance and fulfills its purpose.

At least, for a while. It is inevitable that the balloon will either pop or shrink over time into uselessness and then ultimately be discarded. A balloon has a short life. However, pop the balloon and the air remains unaffected. The balloon drops away and the air remains. It did not diminish or go away, even though the balloon falls away. Instead, the air merges into the atmosphere.

Do you identify with being the balloon or the air? Right now, in your current state, you are both. You are the air and you are the balloon. But just for a while.

Perhaps, like the air, the essence of your self does not go anywhere, nor does it destruct along with the body. The air doesn't die. It is not discarded.

Wouldn't it be great to identify more with the air than the balloon itself?

51
WAVES OF THE OCEAN

We spoke about how grief comes in waves, and how it is best to witness the waves and go with them. Watching waves come to shore can be calming and soothing. Have you ever witnessed how a wave emerges, rolls forward, and then dissolves back into the ocean or breaks along the shore line? Would you ever say that a wave is born, has a life and dies, never to be that exact wave again? Probably not!

When you watch the waves of the ocean disappear, you don't grieve them, nor would you ever think of grieving an individual wave. You know that the wave is clearly part of the ocean. It is not separate from its true nature and nothing is lost when the wave dissolves, merges, and transforms into more waves. Each beautiful wave is never separate from the other waves and all waves are always the ocean.

What would change if we could recognize our true nature as the ocean and could see our individual lives as waves?

How would the grieving process be impacted if we could know that like the waves, we are not separate from one another or the source that we are made of?

COMMUNICATIONS FROM MOM

52
CONVERSATIONS WITH MOMSY

This is the title to my journals that are dedicated solely to conversations with Mom. The journals are made of soft pastel colored handcrafted paper, ribbons and flowers. Mom would love them and they are chosen with her in mind. They are very beautiful. When I am not writing in them, they sit on the altar that I created for her. The *Conversations with Momsy* journals contain a stream of letters written to her. I share everything – my grief and longing for her, as well as my concerns, my questions, my realizations, my joys, and the changes I see in our family. When I sit by the altar and converse with Mom, my experience is that "our special time together" still exists.

Once in a while, and I truly mean only once in a while, I experience her writing back to me. I can never predict when this is going to happen nor can I make it happen, as much as I would like to. Each time it occurs in a similar way. I am in the middle of a sentence, diligently writing my thoughts to her, when I feel a driving impulse to write something different than I am writing. I allow it... and a message that I was not even conceiving of writes itself. My experience is that she literally interrupts what I am saying midway through my sentence and she writes to me something that I may or may not want to hear. Although it is my personal mission to remain in "current relationship" with mom, I am always surprised to receive a communication.

On one such occasion, I was writing a letter to Mom in my journal early in the morning on the second anniversary of when she first entered the hospital. There was nothing extraordinary about this morning. I was telling her the usual about how much I miss her and how I am not the same without her here. She interrupts and this comes out onto the paper instead:

Do not fret over what isn't anymore. It doesn't bring it back.
It is time for you to fully love life again, as you have always loved life.
I love your joy. You have always given so much love and joy to others.
And you were always so happy giving this love. This is how you have always been, even as a young child, and even when you were challenged

in your adolescence with a crippling disease. You never stopped loving life. This has always been your strength. Don't stop loving. Don't ever stop. Do not give up your love of life because it was my time to go. This was my worst fear for you. I had always been afraid that my death would affect you so deeply that your radiance would be diminished.

Do not let it be true. Don't let life's challenges wear down your ability to love. Please, sweetheart, don't let my passing do you in.

That is my greatest nightmare about leaving. Please know that you will feel nearer to me in your joy and love of life than in your regrets and sadness.

Instead of focusing on how you are not the same, be the same.

Be the same, sweetheart. Be your loving, radiant, joyful self.

Please, find your strength again in loving life. Be the same...

Love, Mom

I was blown away. The message hit home. And her message to me to "be the same" did not go unnoticed by me, especially since that is not how I had been holding it. Only Mom could have such a conversation with me. It reminded me of the many times she would lie on my bed to have a talk with me, to give me what she called "constructive criticism." These conversations occurred when she believed I needed to change something. As hard as it was to hear, I had to admit that she was usually right.

This time was no different.

53
MOM VISITS ME

As I said, no matter how much I wanted it, I could not make a visit happen. I asked Mom, again and again, with all my heart, "Please come visit me." I waited. I looked. I searched. I longed.

Only to find disappointment, again and again.

But I never doubted the possibility to be in communication, even if it wasn't happening. I did not move into despair or resignation. I stayed steady in the knowingness that Mom and I are connected, whether I experience "visits" or not.

She came to me one night while I slept, a few months after her departure. It was distinctly different than a dream. We walked hand-in-hand. She showed me her current abode. It appeared as a modern condo in a beautiful European-looking city. It was decorated with big comfortable chairs and sofas with soft, inviting, gorgeous pillows, fantastic art, deep green and rose-colored walls; everything exuded an extraordinary sense of warmth. We discussed ideas for my birthday party to come. I exclaimed to her, "Mom, we thought you were dead!" She smiled brightly and laughed. I loved being with her and I told her that I wanted to stay with her. Without hesitation, she responded with a mother's clarity, "Not for a while. And your dad will come first." We hugged. It is hard to describe how it felt to hug her except to say that it felt exactly like when I hug someone in my waking life, but without the physical body.

When I woke up, I felt disoriented. Then I felt very sad because I'd just spent time with Mom, and I only wanted more. I didn't want to leave her.

When I looked at her pictures on the altar, they seemed especially one-dimensional.

But I was so grateful.

54
MOM SENDS ME A LETTER

A few weeks later, I received an astonishing message from Mom. Again, it occurred while I was sleeping, which is said to be an easier time for souls to make contact. This time I found myself walking down a path in the woods. I saw a journal lying on the ground and ran to it. Eagerly, I opened the journal to find the writing appearing on the pages to look other-worldly, in 3-D, similar to the writing in the beginning of the movie Star Wars, only it was moving horizontally across the page instead of vertically. This is what it said:

Dear Darlene, [that's what she named me at birth]
I hope this letter finds you feeling good. I would like for you to be good with yourself. I am very well, extraordinarily well. I want you to know this. I want for you to hold this time similarly to when you went to college in Arizona. You were off on an adventure. You were going far away from me but it was okay. We didn't see one another often but you knew we were connected. You knew that we would have contact. And, you knew that we would see one another again.
Love, Mom

I had never thought of comparing this time of loss to when I went to college. It was brilliant advice for me because I was never homesick in college, knowing for sure that we would be together again. I went to school across the country from my parents and sometimes many months would pass before we saw one another. But I never had doubt that we would.

It would be typical of Mom to find a moment from the past I could relate to in order to shift my current understanding. She was always very practical with her advice giving – perhaps some things don't change.

55
MOM SURPRISES
ME AT THE POOL

I was having an ordinary day, going to work out at my club and swim my laps. I entered the indoor swimming pool area when I unexpectedly received an undeniable message from Mom, blasted as if it were on a loudspeaker. It wasn't exactly like I heard it with my ears – but rather a resonance of sound vibrations reverberated throughout my whole being. It shocked me because I wasn't even thinking about Mom at that moment, or particularly feeling loss.

Why be so sad if you can know (know, know, know...) that you will absolutely see me again (again, again, again...)?

Whoa. I stopped in my tracks. I sat on the side of the pool in awe. Mom was indeed trying to help me understand something that she was quite clear about. I didn't exactly know what to do with this, so I jumped into the pool to swim my laps. I started talking to her, trying to explain and perhaps even defend how it's not so easy to not be sad on this side of things... She didn't say any more that day.

Another day, Mom visited me again at the pool while I was swimming laps. I will never forget that conversation. Again, I felt the reverberation of sounds throughout my body, almost like a tingling sensation, and I immediately filled with an experience of her love. I seized the opportunity to tell her how much I missed her. Before my mind could ponder what was about to happen, I felt her response in my body as a vibration – a juicy, wholehearted *I love you.* I was in awe, but stubborn, and I responded in a demanding tone, *I miss you,* wanting to hear that she missed me too. But she stuck to her truth and responded with a voluminous *I love you!* I got it! She was not "missing" me. It dawned on me that maybe the experience of "missing" someone is not quite the same over there.

For after all, why would she "miss" me if she is right here with me? Clearly, she does not feel apart from me.

I am nearer than you think, she communicated. She again emphasized, *Enjoy your life! You spend too much time focusing on the suffering on the planet.*

I asked her, "How can I not? It's so intense, the suffering here on this planet."

Her response was clear and immediate. *There has always been suffering on earth and there always will be. The suffering is temporary. Don't let yourself get so heavy with it.*

Then she showed me a painting that actually hung in our living room of the house I grew up in. It's a mysterious painting of the backs of people dressed in dark brown robes with hoods over their heads lined up as they march into a blazing fire surrounded by a dark background. The painting had always intrigued me and now Mom was pointing to it and telling me, *They are lined up to go there and experience everything on earth, including the suffering.*

I had to digest this – souls were lined up to come to the earth plane and experience the suffering that I found to be so heart-wrenching and wrong.

She also tried to prepare me for one of my soul mate dogs' departure. She said, *She is leaving soon to come here. You need to loosen your grip and trust that you really aren't losing her. I am telling you this so that you can rest in this and enjoy your life more.* I tried to remind her about the attachments to loved ones that happen here on this dimension of earth.

But she did not stray from her point.

And I thought again, "Some things don't change."

56

MOM COMFORTS ME

I remember the weekend, a few months after Mom's departure, when I fully faced the changes in my family dynamics that remained in the wake of Mom's absence. Mom was the connective tissue in our family. She somehow wove everyone together. With her gone, I experienced a loneliness that I had never known before in my life.

All weekend long, I cried my heart out. By Sunday night, worn out, I crawled into bed, my mournful heart rendered heavy with a sense of unrequited love. Finally, I fell asleep. Mom came to me and sat right next to me on my bed, with her back leaning against the wall. Clearly in a different dimension and completely opposite to how I would have imagined, she was in black and white. I was right next to her in color. Her presence felt like a blanket wrapping me up, comforted and loved.

I was so happy and grateful to see her. I offered her a plate of food to share with me. She smiled and shook her head *no*. She telepathically communicated, *I don't eat food in that way any more.* Instead, she continued to patiently sit next to me, so that I could absorb her presence. My heartache melted away and I woke up lighter, remembering in detail our time together.

57
MOM COMMENTS ON MY
"THINGS TO DO" LIST

One morning I was walking my dogs in the beautiful woods near my house. My mind was busy with the things I needed to do that day. Then suddenly, out of nowhere, I heard Mom interrupt me and say,

I don't hang around you all the time, even though I am near you. I am not staying around when you are doing your lists. I certainly had my own and know what that is like, to make lists and think they are so important. I spent a lot of wasted time like that. If only I could have known what I know now. Do not spend all of your time on your lists! They do not really matter and they are not what your life is for.

And then, as quickly as it came, the communication stopped and there was nothing more.

I wanted to respond and continue to talk with her. But clearly, the communication was over.

I bet you can guess that I didn't continue reviewing my lists that moment.

I paid attention to the trees surrounding me, to the sound of the brook near by, and to the symphony of birds chirping.

58
MOM SHARES
IMPORTANT INFORMATION

Once again, Mom came to me as I slept. This time I was intensely aware of how strenuous it was for her to appear to me in a way that I would recognize as her.

As she was coming in and out of her form, she was downloading information to me. As I experienced her effort to communicate, I scrambled inside of myself with fear and anticipated guilt that I wouldn't be able to remember what she was telling me, and her efforts would be for naught. The fear literally gripped me throughout the entire communication and it did not let go of me until I actually sat up and wrote everything down.

She was sitting in a log cabin in the mountains. She was talking to me as if she were presenting in a classroom, downloading information that she wanted me to know.

Don't fret about what you haven't experienced in your lifetime. It all gets lived out in time.

I knew she was referring to my feelings about not having children in this lifetime. It wasn't subtle – there was a baby sitting next to me.

Relationships continue to exist. They don't stop evolving when the body drops away. But here, you know that all relationships are equal. Your soul is equally close in relationship with every person you know.

Her last message was also crystal clear: *What you judge, you will live out. Be careful on what you judge.* I immediately reflected on the political leaders whom I was heavily invested in judging at that time – and knew I needed to heed her advice.

And then, everything vanished. She disappeared and so did the log cabin. I opened my eyes to my heart beating faster and a sense of being more informed.

59
MOM GUIDES ME
AWAY FROM GRIEF

It was the seventh year anniversary of Mom's departure. The night before, I had a flying dream. I have had them before but never like this. For the first time, I knew how to soar without touching down on the earth. I also magically knew just how to slightly shift my body to the right or to the left in order to fly in different directions. With a sense of mastery and ease, I soared. It was delightful!

At that time, I was teaching a year long workshop series called *Embodying The Higher Frequency*. The emphasis of this theme was about how to fully show up in life – with impeccability, presence, authenticity, and positive energy. It seemed to me that the dream was somehow connected.

In alignment with the workshop theme, I approached this anniversary differently than I had the preceding years, in which I couldn't stop crying. This year, in meditation, I asked the question, "What is the highest frequency that I can bring to this anniversary?"

Immediately, I heard Mom respond, *Enough time spent on grieving. I want for you to focus on how we are truly one and that there is no real separation between us. I am telling you, we are not separate! I want you to know our Oneness the same way you recently had total knowingness on how to fly.* I was shocked that she referred to my flying dream!

She continued, *Stop focusing on loss. Grieving is based on a sense of separation. It is time to focus on our Oneness.*

Then, as if whispering into a microphone, I heard her speak into my heart, *I am in your form as you are in my formlessness.*

All grief fell away. It was the first anniversary I did not cry the familiar tears of grief. Not one teardrop. Instead, I felt this supreme Oneness. Only Oneness, beyond words. It was something I hadn't so wholly experienced since Mom's leaving.

I stood up from this astonishing meditation, feeling more awake in ways than ever before. I left my house carrying my workout bag, about to hop into the car, when I heard my inner voice say, "Take a walk." *Okay, I am not going to argue with that.* I put my bag back into the house and I was about to walk around the block, when I heard the same commanding voice say, "No, walk up to the shops." I rarely walk in that direction, but once again, I obeyed and walked to the neighborhood shops. The voice continued, "Walk into this store" and so I did. "Go to the middle counter." Although this guided experience felt surreal and a bit strange, I walked directly to the counter, where I laid eyes on a necklace of a blue bird in flight. I immediately thought of my flying dream and Mom's words to know our Oneness the way I knew how to fly. Without hesitation, I bought the necklace of the bird and chuckled because Mom always loved jewelry. I began to leave the store, but instead, again, I heard "Turn to the left." So I did, and before me was an angel wing necklace, and again I heard Mom's voice, *I am in your form; you are in my formlessness.* The angel wing came home with me. Mom not only loved jewelry but she also loved gifting me jewelry and this appeared to still be true.

I wear the wing everyday, remembering Mom's communication.

When people compliment me on it, I say, "Thank you. And my mom has the other one."

I hear in response, "Wow, that is so cool!"

One woman followed that with, "You are so lucky you still have your mom!"

And I sincerely agreed, "I am!"

60
MOM ENLIGHTENS ME

One day, I was walking along when out of the blue I heard Mom clearly say: *The way you know how much you love your life is by how much you enjoy it!*

Being surprised by messages from the beloved who is on the other side transforms the ordinary moment into something magical and mysterious. It never ceases to fill me with awe.

Another day, again out of nowhere, I heard Mom say to me, *You know how after we visit, you experience my photo as one-dimensional and lacking the richness you felt in our visits?* Yes, I knew exactly what she was referring to. *Just like the photos, the common human understanding of "life" and "death" is equally as one-dimensional compared to what it really is. How you think about it is as far from the truth as that photo of me is me.* She further explained, *For the soul, there is not a big differentiation between "life" and "death." The only death that exists is the shedding of the physical body. Consciousness continues, the soul continues, the subtle bodies continue. From a soul's point of view, living a lifetime is similar to you having a dream. And it's not really linear but more parallel, existing all at the same time. When you are on this side of things, you know that discarding the physical body is not a big deal on a soul level because life continues.*

I think I could spend the rest of my life contemplating that message alone. Mom was downloading information to me that was simply her reality and yet utterly profound for me to receive and digest.

As I glimpse into the vastness of her understanding, I experience humility.

61
MOM'S LETTER TO A
WOMEN'S GATHERING

At the tenth year anniversary of Mom's departure, I held a women's gathering to honor Mom and to share her magnificence with others. A week before the gathering, I sat down, prepared to write something, and asked her what she would like to say to the circle of women. Immediately this response came, and it seemed to write itself as it poured out onto the page without pausing. Then as quickly as it began, it just stopped. I wanted to hear more but no more came.

I share it here just as I received it, without edits:

I lived a wonderful life as Lillian Finkler and then as Lee Gouss.

Yet, in my life, I always thought that I could have done better in my jobs.

I know you believe I was a wonderful mother – and perhaps that is all that matters. I certainly know it was the most important thing I did in my life. I loved mothering. It was hard work but the rewards far outweighed the difficulties and heartbreaks that came with it.

Mothering was the joy of my life. It was so easy to love all of you. Truly, a joy. And, I always knew you loved me. In time, I realized that letting you know how loved I felt by you was equally important as me letting you know how much I loved you.

What would I tell your gathering?

What I always tell you: Enjoy your life; this is the most important thing. But I don't mean it like a Hallmark card. It's not just "enjoy life." Truly love your life, because that is all you have. What you have is your life. Enjoy each day as much as possible.

Your sense of enjoyment or lack of enjoyment is what you are left with as an imprint when you depart from your incarnation. It is just like any memory that you now have – you are either left with a sense of pleasure or displeasure, fulfillment or emptiness, warmth or coldness, homey and safe or unsafe and displaced, alive and embraced or small and rejected. Literally, think of something in the past, honey. Anything. What is the feeling you have? It is the same way when you look back at a lifetime.

What is the feeling you have from it?

Everyday you are creating this ambiance of your life.

I liked my life very much. I had a great husband, children, and friends. For me, this is what a great life was about.

You and others always told me that I was beautiful. I could not see that. I felt too modest to embrace such compliments. I thought it would be conceited to believe that I was beautiful. Now I see that these compliments were only made of love and to accept them would have been to accept more love into my life. And to do that I would have had to claim my sense of worthiness. I missed out on that.

I always thought my body could be better. I didn't like my stomach or my thighs. Now I see how silly that was. I sometimes wasted my time on noticing the imperfections about myself rather than the gifts.

I had a wonderful husband. Your dad loved me. I never doubted this. He gave to me everything he possibly could. He took me to places in the world I never even dreamt of seeing. He was a great father. This made me love him even more. He was there for me one hundred percent when my parents got sick and he always went with me to the hospital. Remember I told you about this – a great husband is someone who is there for you when things are hard. Bernie was this. I knew I could always count on him. He was loyal and dedicated.

What would I change? I worried way too much. Worrying doesn't do anything for anyone anywhere, especially the worrier. I worried excessively as if it would make a difference. Although I knew it wouldn't. But now I am certain that it doesn't help at all at any time. It is a complete waste of energy and time.

It was hard for me to understand that things were just how they were. I didn't need to change anything but I didn't know that. I always wanted things to be different – better – especially for you children. Now, I understand how things are exactly as they are, without needing to be different – and that everything will eventually and inevitably be different anyway.

I know, sweetheart that you suffer with all the suffering. I understand. But remember how I told you about how the souls are lined up to experience exactly what you are calling misery and wrong. It is not possible to understand the deep soul agendas that are involved with the experience of suffering. Something else to learn is that you can't change other people's lives. They are not yours to change. All you can do is listen and support.

Another thing I want to address is how I spent a lot of time making lists in my life. They were helpful but I took them too seriously. Now none of what I had on my lists matters. I measured myself by how well I accomplished what was on my list. I needed a list that just had spontaneity and fun on it.

Don't get me wrong. List-making is good. Taking care of business is important or it will take over a life even more. But living each day by accomplishing what is on the list is not what I recommend to anyone.

Instead, pay attention to how rich your life is in every way.

Pay attention to the moments of beauty.

Create time and space for these moments to reveal themselves.

Make sure you are feasting on these moments and allow more and more of them each day.

Make sure you are living what you are meant to be doing. If you feel something strong in your heart, live it out. It is there for a reason.

To know what is in your heart you must listen. You must be with yourself enough to hear. You must not let yourself get caught up in distractions.

There are things that happen in life that hurt. They are meant to be there. They make sense later. I can see why I needed to be lonely at times in my life. Or sad. Or disappointed. I promise you that they don't stay with you forever. If you could know this – how passing it is – then maybe you don't have to be so disturbed by any of it.

Grief is one of these emotions. I know you take it very seriously. Your grief for me. And for many people, animals, and things. You are writing a book on grieving. It is a very important subject. But I do want to tell you that in the bigger picture, where I am now, grief does not take a toll on life in any way, or at least this is my experience. Understand that there is not loss in the way you think there is – nor the sense of

110

separation. I have tried to tell you this many times. There really isn't "gone" or "deceased" or "death" as it appears.

If you could know that truly it is all okay. Those who suffer (and that you suffer with and for) don't suffer forever. Unimaginable beauty and freedom supersede the suffering you witness. If you could know this... you would be happier. You would live happier. This is what I try to tell you. I try to save you from your own suffering. You seem to be pulled to the suffering over and over, believing that it is wrong. The fact is that it is very short lived.

On the dimension that you live, everything is temporary. Everything will suffer. Everything will die. Everything will go through difficulty. That is how it is. But remember, it is truly ephemeral and life doesn't end with that. Life is change including beyond cessation of the body.

Living an earthly life is a wonderful thing. It is important to live it well. To love what you are living.

If you don't love what you are living in general, then you are not doing what you are supposed to be doing with your life.

Part of living a good life is loving the people you are with. And letting them love you. It can be that simple.

Bring beauty into your life. Don't make it so that you are too busy to make things beautiful, decorate, enjoy nice things, notice beauty, indulge in beauty. Beauty can uplift your spirits, literally. Where there is beauty, there is a stirring of the heart. If you truly stop and feel into the beauty, you will touch into the extraordinary of your daily life.

And while on earth, get your hands into life – into the earth, into food, into chalks and paints, anything that is colorful, rich, delicious, substantial. Yes, substantial. That is a remarkable thing about living a life on earth – energy comes together into substance where you can actually get dirty and messy and tangible. Most importantly, remember to enjoy it.

I remember how all the things I had to do, or thought I had to do, took up much of my energy and I got exhausted from it. You saw my exhaustion. I know you did. It is so clear to me now that I got so exhausted because I did not pay enough attention to how amazing every *day was. It can actually feed your spirit if you allow it to.*

I knew you, my children, were amazing, but I got so caught up with providing each of you what you needed that I did not balance enough of my living with just being with you. When you were just playing, I used that time to do my tasks in the house. It would have rejuvenated me to spend more time just being rather than doing.

What would I like for your gathering to hear from me?

I like that you are learning about my life and that Lee Gouss is still alive in this way and mothering all of you. Anyone that my daughter loves, I love. If I could, I would love to have you over to my home. I would offer you cookies and tea or coffee or ice cream or food and sit with you. I would be genuinely interested in knowing about you, about what you care about, about your children, or your interests or your work or your love life. Anything that you would want to share. I would listen with my heart. I would listen to your heart. I would want you to feel cared about and important. I would want to impart compassion to you so that maybe you would be more patient with yourself. I would want to bring you a mother's encouragement so that maybe you would believe in yourself more and go towards your dreams. I would bring my practical sense to you to help you think through things so that you could accomplish your goals and have what you really want in your life. I would want to laugh with you so that you could have a good perspective on things and not "sweat the small stuff." I would want to hold your hand if you needed, so you would know that you have me on your team.

My desire for you in learning more about my life is so that you believe more in yours and have pleasure in living every day, or at least most days.

Love, Mom

EXPERIENCES OF GRIEF
FROM FELLOW
CLUB MEMBERS

BRITT

As Red Dog and I are on the home stretch of our daily hour-long early pre-dawn walk, a Prius goes by and Red Dog becomes very alert and pulls us after it. We start to run and I think, "Me too, Red Dog. Me too. I want it to be Sally in her car." And we run after it together until ...until he smells something and pulls up short. Distracted, he has forgotten the familiar car, and winded, I stop too. This is one of the ways Grief shows up for me. It is a powerful current, constant and dominating the river of emotion always present under and in me. Some cue, a photo, a gesture, a task, a thought, almost anything can be that Prius driving by, and I'm gathered into the dark stormy weather that is my grief. From that point, that current takes me where it will until it spews me out on to some shore of distraction.

The first thing that comes to mind is that grief for me is an identity crisis. I am not the same person. When Sally would go to New England and leave me here for long periods of time, I would describe my experience as that of a planet that had spun out of its gravitational orbit. It would take a while to settle into my own new orbit, but I knew the other planet would return. There was a phantom gravity that I could hold on to. Now that gravitational pull is gone and I am wandering through space, tumbling through time with only a little idea of who I am or may become. For 17 years I was, in large part, Sally's partner. Perhaps my grief as identity crisis is in proportion to how large a part that was.

As part of not being the same person, almost everything has been awkward. This is particularly true of interactions with other people. I find myself somehow surprised when I find out others are as devastated by Sally's death. Grief has made me more self-centered than ever. I think I blunt my awareness of the grief of others so that I don't fall into my own. Ironically, I long for company in the loss and fear it as well. *Just leave me alone. No, come be close to me.*

My grief is suicidal. Not long before I started writing this, I stumbled across Sally's Facebook page, which led me to a photo tribute to Sally. It was overwhelming. Through my moans and wails, I cried out loud: "I can't do this. I can't stand this. I don't want to be here." And I wondered, if I had a gun, would I use it? For the record, I wouldn't. It's just a feeling and it goes away. But that is the dark desperate place grief can take me to.

Grief is a crisis, a trauma, and an opportunity. I fear that not only is it a crisis of identity, but of health. I worry that the stress of this trauma will have long-term negative effects on my health as it has had short-term effects. Ending up in the hospital two days after Sally's death is indicative of the power of emotional stress. There is opportunity as well. The love and support I have received is truly overwhelming. Humbling. I have been told repeatedly that being able to provide support and comfort to me is a gift. I often don't know how to receive this generosity. I don't quite know what to make of it. I know I don't deserve it, and I know that deserving it has nothing to do with it. How else would I know how truly wonderful and giving my friends and family are? As I have fallen down, they have stood up, and have held me and held me up.

Grief is sacred ground that shares space with love. They are bound together. I have lost friends and felt deep loss, but nothing like this. I loved Sally unequivocally. I made a conscious choice to hold nothing back. Maybe this is the love that never dies. The death-defying love we can give to each other. No, it is not death-defying. We do it knowing that our hearts will be broken. But maybe we just don't believe it until it happens... no matter how many times we experience it. And now, knowing that, should I be so lucky as to love again, my heart will be broken again, will I have the will to be so whole-hearted? Is there enough time for me to be rearranged and to love again? It's hard to believe it is possible.

Grief is a thief. It takes time. There is no way around it. It takes part of everyday. Part of me is in a hurry, and I get slammed to the mat every time I try to get out in front of the grief. "Nuhah boy. You're stickin' with me until I let you go." I want to make deals with grief. "When I have cried two gallons of tears, then will I be done?" No deal. Grief makes no deals.

Grief is a teacher and this is what I have learned so far. Identity is both more substantial and malleable than I thought. I could be wrong

115

about this, but there seems to be an opening for some large shift. Whether I want to go through that opening is unclear. But there is no going back. I know in a more visceral way that loss is a fundamental reality of life. I will lose everyone and everything I have ever loved, including my children and myself. This awareness is what makes us human and I can barely stand it... No, in fact I can't bear it, but there it is, and I am devastated by the sadness it engenders in me. On the other hand, this awareness at times makes me cherish this speck of time even more. It makes me believe that as I wake up to this rearranged person that I am becoming, I will somehow not be afraid to love this life all the more. That I will somehow better integrate my mortality into the vitality that is, until it is no more. Sally surely showed me how to do this. That now, finally sharing a real, first-hand knowledge of the loss that goes on around me all the time, I will become more connected to others, more compassionate, more grateful, more alive. One can only hope that this is true.

So, Red Dog and I will keep taking our walks twice a day. He will want to take off after cars that have the same shape or smell as those Sally drove and I will understand. I also understand that my grief is a work in progress. It is a journey that I would not choose, and cannot avoid. I don't see a light at the end of the tunnel, but there is ample light in the tunnel from time to time, and for that I am and will be forever grateful.

LISA

My father died 29 years ago this Father's day. On Father's Day morning June 15, 1985, I received a phone call from my mother at 8:30 in the morning: "Lisa, your father has died." I gasped for air, threw stuff in a bag, and ran to catch the next flight. All I knew was that I had to get to my brother so that we could walk and crawl through this nightmare together.

One year later, my mother came up from Florida for a visit to my home in Atlanta. She observed what I couldn't see, that I had turned my home into a shrine for my father. He was everywhere and on every wall. She said gently, "This is not healthy for you. This will keep you from moving on."

I knew she was right. That day I took almost everything of his off the walls and tabletops and packed his things into boxes.

That night was one of the most incredible experiences of my life. I had the most amazing visit from my father. He came to not only to tell me that he was okay, but to show me as well. He still looked the same, only thinner, and when he greeted me with, "Hello Darling," I cried. He was the only one in my life to call me "darling."

My father asked me to take a walk with him; he wanted to show me something. I was so ecstatic to see him. I happily walked by his side. He took me to a gravesite, and as we stood above this circular gravestone with his name on it, he said, "I am not there. This is not where I live." He continued walking, and I followed. We came upon this beautiful white Grecian home with large windows overlooking the sea. "This is where I live, in this beautiful home. And so you need not worry, I am okay. It is okay to let go; you will never lose me."

I remembered feeling stunned by the beauty of where he lived on this other seemingly worldly plane. And so relieved that he seemed happy and content.

He came to show me this, as his last loving gesture to help me be okay and now to carry him, not through his things, but forever in my heart.

His visit transcended and expanded my awareness of life, and the continuation of life and caring for those we have loved.

JANIE

My grandfather was the patriarch of the family, and I loved him very, very much. Although I always felt that I was his favorite, I found out later that each of his grandchildren believed that they were also his favorite! This is because my grandfather had a way of making us each feel very special.

Although I grew up in Philadelphia and my grandparents lived in New York City, I visited them several times a month. As I got older, my mother would put me on the train or bus to New York City, and my grandparents would meet me at the other end, often arriving at the station an hour early to be sure they wouldn't miss me. So, I spent many weekends alone with my grandparents, who spoiled me with their love.

My grandfather died suddenly in 1972, about a month and a half before I was to be married. His death was extremely difficult for me and for everyone in my family. Because of his death, I had a small and simple wedding. On my wedding day I was excited, although I felt a bit sad and continued to mourn the death of my grandfather. But during the wedding ceremony a wonderful thing happened. As I was standing under the *chuppah* (wedding canopy) with my husband-to-be, I sensed my grandfather standing there right next to me. I didn't see him; instead, I "felt" his presence. I am *sure* that my grandfather was at the wedding ceremony, watching his granddaughter get married.

I felt my grandfather's presence again at the birth of my first child (who would have been his first great-grandchild). This occurred seven years after my grandfather's passing. I had *just* given birth to my daughter when I again felt my grandfather's presence. I am *sure* he was in the delivery room and that he was the first person to see his new great-grandchild.

It is interesting that during both the marriage ceremony and the birth of my daughter, I was not thinking about my grandfather. When I was getting married, I was listening to the rabbi, focused on what he was saying. Immediately after I gave birth I was exhausted and thrilled and totally focused on my new baby.

After both of these experiences I do believe that a person's soul lives on and can "visit" you from time to time, especially in the first few years after death. Even if I can't always feel my grandfather's presence, I do believe that he has witnessed all major events in my life. This is extremely comforting. Instead of feeling sad I am happy knowing that he is always here with me.

JEFFREE

When I contemplate grief, the first thought that arises is how much I miss the ones I loved who have passed on. This grief remains, burns deep in my heart, and is always present whenever I think of these souls I was fortunate enough to encounter. At the age of 53, I have had my share of experiences dealing with the grief of friends and family members who have departed. Particularly, two loved ones come to mind whose death profoundly changed and restructured me forever. One of these people is my friend Doug.

I was in my twenties and in college when I met Doug. Doug was the first friendship I loved. We were close and shared a friendship I believe few are blessed to have in a lifetime. We had even spoken of the inevitability of our deaths and made a pact together: whoever passed on first would attempt to contact the other from the other side. It was a fascinating thought for us both, and one I did not think I would experience so soon, as Doug passed away when he was only twenty-four. Somehow he had gotten hold of a gun and shot himself in the heart.

When Doug died, it was sudden, and I was immediately grief stricken. It was an explosive and abrupt reality change. The whole world as I perceived it was fundamentally, forever altered. Doug, my dear friend, was gone. It took a long time for me to get over the shock of his death. After the initial emotional trauma, grief took its place. Of course, at the beginning, it consumed me. I was enveloped in an abyss of emotional loss. Who would I talk to like I did to Doug? Who would I share all the memories with we had together other than Doug? Who would appreciate and see me like Doug did? Who would ever know what Doug and I shared and experienced together now that he was gone? Who could I ever again have that special friendship with other than Doug? So many losses all at once.

Grief became a full-time emotional experience and I was lost in it. Lost in grief and lost within myself. When Doug died something inside of me did as well. There was the unforeseen realization that buried within me was a feeling of isolation, because who could possibly know and truly acknowledge the friendship Doug and I shared. The grief around Doug's death left me heartbroken with many feelings I had to reconcile, ultimately and completely by myself.

Yes, I had a wonderful support system of family and friends but no one could go to that place of grief I was in and meet me there. If I was to move forward, I had to find "the way," my way. If only I was in charge of how long my grieving would take I would have stopped it sooner. Oh the pain, the pain! I have learned grief takes its time and there are simply no shortcuts. In my experiences of grieving around the death of a loved one, I've realized it is an emotional ride that in some ways never completely ends. I am left to take that ride whether I want to or not all while attempting to simultaneously learn how to move on with the life before me.

Grief over the loss of Doug turned to despair. The first two to three weeks after, I just wanted to be alone. Who could understand what loss I felt? Alone I felt, alone I hurt, alone I missed, alone I cried, and alone in my grief I ultimately was. I would not feel so much loss if I did not feel so much love for the friendship we shared, for Doug! Within my grief and despair I felt my connection to Doug.

Alone and in my home, I sometimes found myself talking to Doug even though he was not physically there. I spent my time reflecting on the friendship we had. I picked up the guitar and sang songs we had sung together. I thought of all his qualities I admired. I then decided to draw, something Doug was very good at. I picked up a pencil and drawing pad and gave myself permission to give it a go. Within a few minutes I found myself drawing in much the same way Doug did and yet with a very distinct style that was my own.

One drawing after the next appeared and I was amazed! I was never able to draw like this before! It was like something was coming through me and I was its vehicle. I had no idea where the drawings were coming from, nor did I care. I just wanted to keep drawing. I remember being able to visualize what I wanted to draw on the paper before I had drawn it. This continued to happen for about seven days. I still have those drawings today, all fifteen. I have never been able to draw like that again.

It wasn't until many months later, after I had this drawing experience, when I remembered Doug and I had made our pact: whoever passed on first was to make contact with the other here on Earth. I knew Doug

121

kept his word through those drawings and that we connected to each other beyond this earthly life.

Along with this realization, I began to become aware of an inner peace. This coupled with an inner knowing I was mindful of more than ever: there is more to this life than meets the eye. I have no desire to prove or convince anyone of my experiences. I can only say grief led me there.

Although I still live the grief of Doug's passing, time has healed much. From the bottomless burning that comes with grieving, through the passage of time, these experiences have given me timeless gifts. Gifts that come in the form of embracing this life and those around me with an impassioned presence. To give, to love myself and others while I'm alive and still can, always with awareness of the stark reality that there is death and there is grief and there is life itself that marches on.

ELLEN

June 20, 2012. That's the day that everything changed. That's the day Daniel left at age 28 and never came back. He went to sleep and never woke up. Now I never wake up from the nightmare that is life without him.

Those first few months seemed improbable. My grief felt raw, so consuming, so limitless in its pain. It crushed me slowly from the inside out. I wept with such passion and ferocity, it felt literally suffocating. I struggled to find acceptance in his death and felt guilty when I no longer cried every day. I feared I would forget the lines of his face, the crackle of his laugh, the color of his eyes just before he cried. I've learned to let go of the need to contain my grief, and the need to make sense of it. I write letters to him, which contain the tiny details I never want to forget. And slowly I've learned to make space for things in my heart other than Daniel.

I live my life to honor him. I love to honor him. I thrive, so his memory thrives as well.

Grief is seismic. It shifts your soul and your universe. Grief makes the triviality of life fall away, and refocuses the heart and mind on what really matters. For me, that meant spending more quality time with the people I love most. Had I been more present with Daniel, would he still be here today? I'll never know. Yet in my grief, and in my growth from grief, I found the courage and the honor to leave a heartless career to embark on a new one that affords me time and genuine presence with the people I love.

My grief also shifted my idea of what it means to give and accept help. I am quick to give of myself, while not being mindful to replenish my resources. In my grief, I felt raped of any ability to care for myself or others, and for the first time I surrendered into receiving the outpouring of love and support with open arms and a raw, weeping heart. My loved ones stood up as I crumbled. They held me when I had no strength to hold myself. They remain my refuge, my compassion, and my release.

I've soaked in years of therapy, love, and support, and countless conversations with Daniel. I speak, and he listens. I hear the silent, resonate echo of his acceptance and his love. Talking to him remains equally difficult and cathartic. The tears never cease to flow, the pain never seems to end. But slowly and surely, I learn to breathe a little deeper and smile a little more often. Love is the silver lining of my grief. Love for Daniel, and the love of those around me. It wraps and warms the soul. It shines through the darkest days and brings life to the most impossible moments. I grieve Daniel openly and gladly, because someone so worthy of such love is worthy of beautiful grief.

SHAUN

It is impossible to quantify the magnitude of grief and the presence it carries, an everlasting scar from the moment it intrudes. Real grief, not temporary sadness, but deep, deep grief, shatters one's world and leaves a trail of life's pieces in its path.

The initial gut-wrenching sucker punch that grief inflicted on me is a horror of indescribable pain that has subdued, in time, into an integrated component of the many facets of my life.

Time heals all wounds, but all wounds forever leave inflicted damage. I *grieved* my father. Eighteen months later, I'm not so sure I associate the feelings I have with true grief, but rather emotions like sadness, disbelief, and regret. For me, true *grief* were those first weeks following the action that gave birth to my *grief*. A year and a half ago, my father lost his life to the consuming mental illness of depression, in which he was overcome with darkness and irrationally. He lost his battle with this devastating illness by suicide. We were on a family vacation, grandkids and all, and it was the last day of the trip, when we awoke and he was not in the condo; never would we suspect his ill fate, until the booming deepening sounds of *KNOCK, KNOCK* echoed in the condo coming from the front door. It had that unfamiliar sound of panic. When I opened the door, several police officers stood at the door, and instantly a sickening feeling came over me, and I just knew. As they spoke, time froze, and the dark character of *grief* had a first-class ticket into my own life – and the lives of everyone ever touched by the amazing person my father is.

The initial grief was shocking, numbing, surreal, suffocating, and omnipotent. There was no escaping it, in my waking state or in my dreams, and no real answer to damper it or try to extinguish it. When one loses a loved one – in my case a father – to the instantaneous death of suicide, one is left with no answers. Like floating in space, there is nothing to grab onto that seems concrete.

My father was stripped from my life with no forewarning, no opportunities to say goodbye, and no directions to answer the extreme unknowns associated with any form of sudden death, and of course, the further black hole of unknowns associated with suicide.

Like depression, an internal illness of the mind, the grief became my internal struggle. Unanswered questions, as well as the reverberations from the immediate shock and impact of sudden loss, haunted me. The old saying "hindsight is twenty-twenty" earned crystal clear meaning. Did we miss the signs? Did we do all that we could do? Were my final interactions and moments with my dad of love and in the present? These are questions that go hand-in-hand with the grief that will forever be open-ended. In my grief, my mind could not stop asking questions such as "How could he?" "Why did he?" and "What triggered such an impulsive decision?" All are without answers except for that which remains forever buried with his last breath and will forever haunt my consciousness. And even my own interpretation of the situation is nothing more than a story I have written in my head as a possible truism. But I realize it's only my own created story and likely not the real reason or answer to my endless list of questions. So I digress, but I will never forget the waking nightmare of the first 24 hours and how painful that first week was, tormented with the mental agitation and a breaking heart.

Following the funeral, my grief began to shift, which was almost relieving. By the end of the second week, I no longer found myself crying to sleep every night or waking up to my tears every morning. I didn't cry every time I pulled up to the driveway of my parents' home for the last 25 years; my home that I grew up in. I think the fact that my immediate family and I spoke constantly (consuming, really) and honestly about our emotions and the possible events that led to the unfathomable death allowed myself to move past the immense grief phase more quickly. We left it on the table with nothing to hide from each other.

Although there was a slow metamorphosis in my grief, my world still felt frozen in agony while the rest of the world kept moving, kept breathing, kept rotating. So, I focused on helping my mom, helping to streamline the daunting list of to-dos that now fell on her shoulders. My grief existed, but it also began to bury itself into a nook of my soul that would stay there then, now, and forever.

I now had to try and fill part of my Dad's shoes. Mainly, the focus of my grief shifted to my mom, who lost her husband of nearly 40 years, her college sweetheart, her companion and partner in life that been by her side for more than 4 decades! And for my sister, already at a tender age of mid-20s, trying to find her way in the real world, and who had now lost the largest male influence in her life. The way that I held it was that I lost my dad and my best friend, but I still had family and my own family – my wife and two amazing kids. Their laughter and innocence served as my only antidote to the grief, but my mom lost her life partner and my sister lost her Daddy – and now both were alone to an extent. I grieved for them in not only their loss of a loved one but the pain I knew they felt that I, nor anyone, could fix. It's the most helpless feeling, because once grief is born, like life, it doesn't end until death.

No matter how much I learn to live with grief and how much it may subside in time, I experience loss as always there. It makes its presence known, even for a short second with a memory of my dad or when I go to a favorite place or restaurant I enjoyed with him. As time has passed, I don't grieve him constantly, but there are countless moments where I deeply miss him or grieve the lost opportunities together – sometimes the trivial ones more so than the big ones. I grieve the fact that I feel cheated; my mom was cheated; my siblings cheated; my kids cheated; and he was cheated, all by a terrible disease. I grieve all the memories he is missing in all of our lives and how much he would have beamed with joy had he been here. I grieve not being able to talk to him on the phone or grab lunch with him on a random Tuesday. I grieve his voice and his embrace. I grieve that unbreakable family bond we shared in Atlanta that made our small Atlanta family feel so large and present. I grieve that my son will never know first-hand how amazing his grandfather was. I grieve that my daughter lost her best friend.

Each person's grief is their own and no two forms of grief are the same or will follow a similar healing path, for everyone's situation is different. Life is not perfect; I always knew that, but now I know it more than ever. Life is complicated and painful at times, but it's beautiful too. And while I grieve the loss of my dad and the unrealized memories that were never shared, I also appreciate more than ever the 33 years I shared with him. My grief at times gives me greater appreciation for the things I can no longer grab onto. The life opportunities and gifts that he gave to me and the morals he passed on to me are what my wife and I ensure our kids honor and live by.

Survivor? I know that's what I am labeled. But I am not a survivor. I am simply a son living life how his father would have hoped had he still been here. I am a father, son, and brother trying to keep our family bonded by the unconditional love he instilled in all of us.

I'm not a survivor, I'm just me. I love you, Dad.

RENEE

I am grieving my brother, Todd, who was killed by a drunk driver. At first I was incredibly angry, and remained stuck in a place of rumination about how unfair it was. During this time I was not well, and was very destructive. One day, by grace, this just shifted, and I "got" on another level that I had not been on previously – a realization that this wasn't bringing him back, and instead, it was keeping me in a horrible place. It was serving only to make me unhappy, and I could not remain here any longer. I was also in this horrible place, because it felt like to accept his death – to not be resistant and think of how unfair it was – would be accepting and saying I was okay with what happened.

After I got through that stage, it was very healing to spend time with his close friends who he and I grew up with. It was also incredibly healing for me to talk about him and my grieving process with people who were grieving too, and/or had lost someone they loved. When I talked to people who had not lost anyone yet, I felt alone, misunderstood, and generally unseen. This was a very lonely and isolating experience. Writing and talking to Todd also helped me to feel our connection.

Losing my brother changed me in many ways. I nest and stay home more. I still can't handle a lot of overstimulation. I could've gone out almost every night before the accident, now I struggle if I have plans more than a couple of nights a week. I need more alone time. Any kind of stimulus can be hard, even if not too excessive (like bright light, noises, people talking).

I also now have a very low tolerance for friends who don't really come through for me and show love and support. I've ended quite a few relationships since the accident. On the other hand, I feel a deepening of other relationships with loved ones who really do come through. I appreciate and value these relationships even more now. I also am a lot more intolerant to drama and unhealthy relationships.

I have grown, and value people and life more, take less for granted, and don't get caught up in being upset by little things. I also now can provide support to others in a more multi-layered and rich way than I previously could.

I learned that I can endure and make it through unbelievably heartbreaking and horrible tragedy, and I feel stronger than before.

I feel altered in a way that I'm unsure how to describe with words. It's like some of my innocence has been ripped away. A permanent change that I know will always remain.

Today, as I write this, I experience what I know a lot of people do: times I'm okay or happy, then waves of despair, then sometimes anger. It changes often and comes in waves. It's helped me to know this is how it is, and I can't control it, and to know grief isn't a linear process. That there's nothing to move past or get over, just to take life moment by moment, accept what I'm feeling and experiencing, and ride it out.

DEVAJOY

The following are passages excerpted from my memoir *Stripped to the Core: A Daughter's Experience of Her Mother's Descent and Transition*. I share this in honor of my Mom's spirit as well as to connect with others who know the painful process of sitting vigil and letting go.

Grief had already stripped me of my defenses, made me raw and vulnerable, and in reverie the naked vitality of the world assaulted me. In these moments, I no longer had the armor of my ideas about things and the world. I was no longer able to make sense of things, I could only sense them.
— Robert Romanyshyn

Mom had one of the worst descents I have ever witnessed or even heard of. Fifty-five days of hell. Unable to breathe on her own, her lips swollen, her mouth parched like in the blazing heat of desert sun, the ventilator invades her throat and insides. With tubes attached everywhere into her nostrils and both arms, the veins become tired, bruised and sore from being stuck too many times. Time ticks ever so slowly in the hospital. Day after day, she lies there with little responsiveness. Yet, at night, she flails her arms and legs and they tie her down, and nothing is worse then walking out of the room to leave her tied down against her will. While sitting vigil, there is a deep sorrow throughout the ICU unit. "Depressing" is too mild of a word to describe the pain that pulsates from each corner and crevice of the ICU hospital unit. The vulnerability and mortality of the human condition is on a loudspeaker everywhere you turn. You can't get away from the sense of intense heartache.

Time is punctuated by the brief moments when an attendant comes in and checks on her. A nurse makes an appearance to check the monitor. And then, finally, the long awaited monumental moment happens when the doctor actually arrives – for a minute. There is the monotony of the lunch break. Everything is in slow motion: the pushing of the elevator button, the stepping into the elevator, the elevator taking me away for a moment in time from the floor that houses the horrific destiny, the elevator door opening, stepping out of the elevator and pointing myself to the less than appealing cafeteria that now becomes a refuge. It offers me a breather from being in face-to-face contact with the nightmare of loss. Time for tears, time for some calls to friends, time to look at something else besides the heartbreaking fate of my mom and all of us who love her.

Anyone who has been there, at a hospital stay during the descent of the beloved, knows that the passing of time is completely different than in ordinary life. I have a ritual of looking up at the sky right before I walk into the hospital. Daylight. Sky. Morning. Hello, day. And... *goodbye*, day. Pass by the security desk and see the same faces every day. They greet us with empathy and familiarity as the days become weeks become months. Every moment is surreal and sketched into my memory. Walking through the repetitive rituals of each day in slow motion – this time pushing the elevator button to take us up to the floor where my mom lies with a ventilator in her mouth and a food tube in her stomach, to our destination where our hearts will stretch as far as they can as we hold Mom's hands in these last days that they can be held.

Stepping out of the elevator, we courageously walk into the day's hell. Dad with his newspapers in hand, my sister, Donna, with her book and a bag filled with lotions, nail polish, and perfume for Mom with hopes that perhaps this is the day she could magically give Mom a break from the slow decay of her body. I carry my bright pink backpack that weighs a ton, filled with way more books than I could read, my journal, pens, magic markers, bottles of water for everyone, cell phone chargers, and a bag of chocolate covered pretzels that will be eaten for momentary escape.

Time is not a road – it is a room.
— John Fowles

There is the moment of turning into her room and entering our saddest place on planet earth. Although it is late morning, she is lying there, still tied down from the night before. Seeing Mom tied down is a nightmare. She can only move the right side of her body but the ropes rob her of even that. Mom's skin tones are changing into a pale paste and weird colors that one never wants to see in anyone they love. Her poor mouth... The suspension of water or even ice over these long weeks leaves her mouth parched, lips cracking and bleeding and looking so painful. Her beautiful white teeth that sparkled when she flashed her big gorgeous smile are now grey and brown and decaying with a stench that cannot be ignored. My sister, who has a hypersensitive sense of smell, is immediately sick to her stomach from the smell of toxins and decay being expelled by our mother's body that we can't do anything about.

As people walk by my mother's room and peek inside, their eyes catch a glimpse of a devastating ghastly sight of a person in tremendous crisis. I watch them and sense their relief that this is not their mother. I don't blame them.

I just can't believe it is mine. My radiant mom who was in her house and having a life just a few days ago, who was on the phone with me, sharing and laughing, who was making plans for our next rendezvous, a trip to New York City together, just a few weeks from now .We planned this trip for after her exploratory surgery by the doctor – which she failed to mention was an *oncologist* gynecologist. No one prepared us for the possibility of strokes that occurred one-by-one during and after her surgery that would end all plans, all trips, all of everything.

Mom has better days than others, measured by the level of agitation she seems to suffer. Each of us tries to make ourselves useful. I think our actions are more for us than any relief they truly bring to Mom. We adjust the pillows; we brush her hair; we apply lotion to her skin; we attempt to clean her mouth; we run for the nurse to do this or that; we keep her favorite music playing that I grow to be so sick of and will probably never want to hear again. We talk to her; sing to her; read to her; comfort her; comfort ourselves; we barricade ourselves from the nauseating reality of our beloved dying – with nothing to really do to stop or even relieve her suffering at all.

Time to plant tears, says the Almanac.
— Elizabeth Bishop

Time passes. Each day. In this way. The sun goes down. A beautiful sunset in a winter sky. Grateful for it being winter with ice and snow and freezing cold, an exact match for how I feel inside of myself.

We prepare to leave, so we can get some supposed rest, so we can return again with renewed energy for meeting today's hell again tomorrow. This is the schedule Dad has set up for himself and us.

We want to leave. We don't want to leave. It is so hard to leave. Please don't tie down my mom. No, please don't. I don't want to leave if it means that she is tied down. Dad's exhaustion is palpable – "Come on, let's go" – and I take a deep breath. We say things like "We love you Mom." "We'll be back tomorrow, Mom." "We pray you rest through the night." We know our words don't bring any relief. She is in this alone. We put on winter coats, hats, and scarves that Mom will never wear again. We grab our things. We kiss her one more time. She does not respond. We take leave of the room that we will return to all too soon and not soon enough. Back to the elevator that delivered us so many hours ago. Feels like such a long, long day. Tears in eyes, we are so drained. Exhausted from sitting and standing all day in the stuffiness of a hospital room, the heart is the only muscle we have stretched.

With little to say to one another, we ask one another, "Where shall we eat tonight?" Eating is our attempt to normalize ourselves and it's so hard. It doesn't stop being hard. We walk past the security guards and out through the hospital doors into the night. I look up into the dark night sky and look for the moon that will orient me to the passing of time. I take a deep breath of the cold air in hopes of releasing the day's heaviness, knowing that I can't.

I don't know who it is who lives or dies, who rests or wakes, but it is your heart that distributes all the graces of the daybreak in my breast.
– Pablo Neruda

The next day, a breakthrough happens. February 15, Mom's Valentine's Day gift to me that I will never forget. I am standing by her bed. Her eyes open and she reaches her one mobile hand out to touch my face. Her fingers caress my cheeks as my tears run down them. My cheeks that never thought they would feel her touch again. My heart quivers as I receive what feels like the most delicious, magnificent touch I will ever experience.

Again and again on this day, she looks toward me, reaches her hand to me and intentionally brings her love to me. She reaches for my necklace and touches it for a moment. She reaches for my sweater to fix it from hanging off my shoulder, as only a mom would do. She reaches for me to bring me close to her in an embrace. Oh my God, Mom is hugging me. There could be no more beautiful hug than this. Eternal moments. Delicious moments. She is actually looking into my eyes. I do not know what she sees or comprehends but I know that Mom is communicating her love to me!

Staring into my eyes, she reaches her hand to my chest and taps right on my heart approximately twenty times with a fist that feels deliberate and strong. She is intently telling me something. I hear her.

I love you. I love you so much. You must be strong in the love.
I am so proud of you. Know this! Love is inside of you.
You must be strong in love.

I will never forget this. I will never forget, Mom...
This was the greatest Valentine's Gift of my life.

In grief I was forced to come to terms with the brutal fact that I am not really in control of my life, and that no matter what I might do I cannot save anyone from their fate, least of all those whom I love. Grief blew apart my familiar world and forced me to recognize that I am not as much the author of meaning as I had believed myself to be.
— Robert Romanyshyn

Forty days into it, agitation increases with intense discomfort. She no longer reaches out. She is done. Obviously done. But her body is not. Once in a while, her life energy peeks enough to try to wiggle out of the ropes around her ankles. There is no difference for her between the day and night, except that she is alone and tied down at night. While my sister, dad, and I are home trying to sleep, we try not to think of her lying in that cold hospital room, tied down, alone, dressed in a diaper, hospital gown and tubes. Time keeps ticking. We can't get away from thinking about her.

As time moves us deeper into the intolerable, Mom is able to express her preferences and dislikes. This night, the last night before life supports are removed, Dad starts into the evening ritual of tying her ankles down. Furiously, she moves her legs and growls right through the tracheotomy tube and right through the fog of the stroke. It is clear what she is saying. Dad insists it is for her safety.

I cannot watch. I have to walk away. I am horrified. I am betraying her by not stopping him. *I am so sorry, Mom,* I want to scream out. It is all so wrong, so wrong! What is wrong with us? *Please forgive me, Mom.*

Tying Mom down might make rational sense but my whole being is screaming, screaming out "NOOOOOOO!" It is *her* "no!" It is *my* "no!" Despite our congruence, it remains a silent "no."

Do not let what you cannot do interfere with what you can do.
— John Wooden

It seems like each time everyone leaves the room to take a break, Mom communicates to me. She is lying still in some sort of sleep state but quickly after others take leave, she starts tossing and trying to communicate what feels like soul agitation. Attempting to get out of the bed, she is silently screaming, "I want to leave! Get me out of here, now!" She is trying to stand and march out of the room forever. I know her legs can not hold her up With all my might, I wrap my arms around her, trying to pull her back to lying down, and call out to her, "Mom, stop! Please stop!"

She is communicating to me, her daughter who she trusts to understand what she needs. She takes the one hand that can now move and tries to tear off her wristband, then her robe, and then almost violently rolls herself from one side of the bed to another in utter

136

turmoil. Her agitation increases to such a high shrill of intensity that she tears at her breast, as if attempting to get out of her body.

Amidst all of the commotion, we have a very powerful exchange. For a moment, we hold eye contact. With intensity I ask her, "Mom, do you want help to go?"

She stares at me. With total intention, to communicate, she hits the side of the bed with her one hand that is able to move, and then extends her arm up toward the ceiling and shakes it with exasperation as if to exclaim to the gods above, *What do you think? What else can we do? Do something to stop this misery now! That is the only thing to do, don't you see?*

When I was a child, kids picked on me at school. When my suffering became too much, Mom couldn't stand it anymore and would declare "Enough!" Then, with conviction, she would proceed to call the parents of the children with a hope to stop my suffering. Although it was embarrassing, I felt protected and loved. Now, our roles are reversed and it is time for me to step up to the plate and make this insanity stop, to declare, "Enough!"

Her loud yet silent scream reverberates inside of me and in reaction I cry out, "Mom!" The agitation actually pauses and again, she looks me in the eyes for a moment. I know that we are communicating. With all of my might, I exclaim to her, "Mom, this is it! This is your last night doing this! It's over! I promise you! No more of this!"

It is the most intense promise I have ever made.

I am ready to meet my Maker. Whether my Maker is prepared for the great ordeal of meeting me is another matter.
— Winston Churchill

That night, I convince my dad that it is time. Life supports are removed. With a sense of relief beyond words, I believe this is the beginning of the end of the suffering.

As she lies there, I can hear her voice inside of me.

I am raw. There is nothing else but raw. I am sick.
There is nothing else but sick. I am decaying.
There is nothing here but decay.
I am wailing as I have never wailed before.
No one hears me.
This body is no place to be.
It is now between me and my Maker.
Take me... take me...
What's taking so long?
Why do you make me suffer so?
There is no choice but to wait...

We are all waiting. Waiting...

The present is the only thing that has no end.
— Erwin Schrodinger

Dad, my sister, and I are sitting vigil this night. We are not going home. Her ankles are not tied down. The tubes are gone. We sit. In the dark. Even the hospital corridors are quiet. Mom is sleeping soundly, and so is Dad in a chair next to her.

I watch them sleeping side by side, the first time in forty-five days, the last time in their fifty-five years together. I gaze upon them being as close to one another as they can be. There is nothing more poignant than this moment for me as I watch them sleep into the night together. Dad's mouth drops open as sleeping mouths do; Mom's small body seems more peaceful, perhaps even comforted by the familiar snoring sounds. As I am allowed into their private space together, there is something achingly beautiful and holy about this moment... something I yearn to preserve forever.

The Friend, who knows a lot more than you do, will bring

difficulties, and grief, and sickness, as medicine, as happiness, as the essence of the moment when you're beaten, when you hear Checkmate, and can finally say, "I trust you to kill me."
— Rumi

It didn't go as I hoped. These final days without life support are not like in the movies or my fantasies. My commitment to Mom to stop the suffering is not a success and it was out of my control. Mom's agitation continues to ebb and flow, sometimes with great intensity. We can only powerlessly watch and hope for her not to linger a moment longer. My sister and I find ourselves pouncing on the nurse if she offers to give Mom aspirin, questioning whether the pills will prolong her life. I hear myself begging, "Make it stop. Make this be the last time she feels pain. Please, please, please, no more pain." I am intensely praying and I have no idea to whom.

The doctor says that it takes three days and nights for the body to starve and dehydrate enough of all of the nutrients and water and then maybe a day or two more. It is a strange thing to be counting the days, counting the moments, to when someone you love so dearly dies.

Time is a great teacher, but unfortunately it kills all its pupils.
— Hector Berlioz

Twenty-four hours, no food or drink...
Forty-eight hours, Mom's body is dehydrating...
Seventy-two hours, Mom lies still like a corpse, but her skin is still warm...
Agitation increases. it gets bad...
We try to soothe her, encourage her towards the light, give her permission to leave, say all the right *Kubler-Ross* things to say...
One hundred and four hours pass...
Days come and go...
I try everything. The mind starts to go a little crazy. Maybe she will let go today if I wear my underwear with blue sky and clouds on it. The

139

sky, the clouds, maybe...

No, that doesn't work.

The next day. Maybe it will work if I wear my *Winnie the Pooh* underwear because she has a thing about *Winnie the Pooh* and doesn't like him. Well, really only because my brother never outgrew his relationship with *Winnie the Pooh*. So, maybe... Nope, the day and night go by and I take off my *Winnie the Pooh* underwear, without any results. That didn't work.

In meditation, I visualize cutting the cords between Mom's physical body and ethereal energy body with a golden scissor. I tell Donna about the inspirational idea to cut the cords to set Mom free. To my surprise, the next day she marches into Mom's room and immediately Donna's fingers take the shape of a scissor, and she starts to fiercely cut the cords as efficiently as she can! It is actually hysterical, if only it isn't so sad. When she is done, a minute later, she turns to me and declares, "That didn't work!" I attempt to explain to Donna, "In my meditation, the cutting of the cords was done slowly and mindfully with deep intention." She looks back at me with wide eyes that speak of the desperation we both feel. I proceed to slowly imagine the cords and with deep breaths, slowly cut while whispering, "It's okay to let go! .Let go..."

Later that same day, with Mom lying in the bed looking like a breathing corpse, my sister turns to me with exasperation and exclaims, "I think we need a bigger scissor!"

"Don't just do something," Buddha said, *"stand there!"*
— Daniel Berrigan

Sitting vigil is probably the most intense experience of my life. Seemingly perfect moments for her to depart would come and go. Appearances of perfect expressions of love, perfect sunsets, perfect completions. Again and again. I kiss her face everywhere, ever so softly, wholeheartedly. I breathe breath into her third eye point in the middle of her forehead and then gently bring my lips to hers. I want to be here with her as one of the last faces she sees, as she was the first face I saw upon arriving. I tell her that I want her to be the one who greets me when I cross over. I tell her that she has been the greatest mother. I encourage her to go. It is clear that it doesn't matter what I say. She remains here.

When I finally give that up, and I am quiet, she is relieved. *Ah, finally...*

(Months later, after her departure, Mom communicates with me that it was really annoying to hear me repeatedly say, *It's okay to let go, it's okay, let go!* She declared, *Don't you think if I could have, I would have!*)

Death is just infinity closing in.
— Jorge Luis Borges

It is the 51st day of her descent and Mom is finally being moved to the hospice floor, away from the obnoxious sound of the hospital construction work being done right next to her room. What a relief to get away from that daily pounding that added to our nightmare!

Somehow the changing of the rooms breaks a trance that Donna and I have been in, and it dawns on us to bring Mom her own pillow and favorite blanket from home. "How could we have not thought of this earlier?" we question one another with shame and remorse. It now feels like this simple but immensely important action has just been waiting for us to break from the spell and we cannot tolerate another moment for Mom to be without her own pillow. Like the speed of light, we rush home with urgency to gather what now feel like sacred objects. We arrive back at the hospital at sunset time. It is 6:00 p.m. March 4 as we place her pillow under her head. Remarkably, her body *immediately* stops breathing. Everything is still. The moment feels like an eternity, as we watch with astonishment. Oh my god, her pillow took her home!

And then, as we feel suspended in time, we see her breath breathe her body, again.

Tonight will not be the night. We kiss her goodnight. We approach the elevator. Simultaneously, a little girl steps into the elevator with us, holding a woman's hand. The girl is screaming, "I want my Mommy! I want my Mommy!" as she stares into my eyes the whole elevator ride down. All six floors. This is one of those "movie moments." My own inner little girl is screaming on the top of her lungs right in 3D in front of me. My sister takes my hand.

I found out that the little girl's mother was in labor with her soon-to-be little brother. If only our story was nearly so kind.

We step out of the hospital to be met by cool air. As we exhale, the night sky cloaks us in a blanket of darkness, wrapping us in a chilling sense of the unknown.

Never place a period where god has placed a comma.
— Gracie Allen

March 5th. There is a shift. How strange, I am not drawn to approach Mom. She lies there like a shell, an empty shell. No one is home, except for the breath. As Donna and I take a walk, circling the hospital parking lot for the fifth time, she ponders out loud, "Do you think Mom's soul left her body last night when her head made contact with the pillow and that's why we don't feel like she's there?" As soon as she says the words, there is no doubt inside of myself. This is exactly what has happened. She is no longer there. Just her breathing corpse.

No light born in love can ever be extinguished.
— Darcie D Sims

The night before the 55th day of descent, the 10th day off of life support, I have a dream of a long and slender man strangely dressed in a dark suit. He walks into the middle of my ordinary dream and turns directly to me as if on center stage and I am the audience. He clearly announces, "She's gone!" Immediately I wake myself up and with urgency, I dial the hospital with shaking hands. So typical, the response to my urgent plea to check in on Mom was to put me on a long hold that seemed to last forever. Finally, a woman on the other end of the phone says, "She is still breathing."

We walk into her room to see Mom laboriously breathing; her body is working strenuously to simultaneously shut down and stay alive. We can only stand by and watch. The day is sprinkled with visitors. It's around 5:00 p.m. and I am chanting softly into Mom's ear. Mom's closest girlfriends come to visit and Dad is down the hall talking to someone. I think to myself, "This is a chance to surround her in a sacred circle of feminine energy." I don't say anything but I picture us holding hands around Mom and invoking presence, love, and beauty. Right at this moment, the women encourage my sister to sit with them near the window away from Mom's bed. I let go of my idea as I turn to stare out the window at a lovely sunset painted with wispy grays, pinks, and blues. My eyes follow the arc of a bird's flight across the pastel sky until it is no longer visible. As it disappears from my sight, my eyes shift back to Mom and it is this moment that she takes her very last breath.

It is a sacred moment that will last my lifetime.

I call for my sister. She joins me by Mom's bedside.

Free at last. At this moment, there are no tears. Just silence.

We return to our home in the darkness. The vigil is over. We approach the house to see a family of at least six deer in our driveway. Deer, Mom's favorite animal and Spirit symbol. In awe, we enter the house quietly, so as not to scare the deer away. We don't want the deer to ever go away.

The presence of that absence is everywhere.
— Edna St. Vincent Millay

The act of opening my eyes every morning into another day to find this hollowness inside of myself feels like I am moving through molasses. Each day is extremely challenging to get through. Another day without my Mom on the planet. My family, never again the same.

As time passes, I find that I no longer place flowers on Mom's altar every week as I once had. But the altar remains in tact and only expands

143

with gifts that I still give to her. The shock is occasionally still there. The depth of my sorrow doesn't lessen; the *Noooo* still screams out within myself. Just when I think I am moving through the grief to the other end of the tunnel, another trigger for the wave of grief happens and linear time falls away, leaving me naked all over again, sometimes on my knees crying. But not all the time. Sometimes I can feel her so strongly with me that I literally do not experience her as gone.

Eternity is not something that begins after you're dead. It is going on all the time. We are in it now.
— Charlotte Perkins Gilman

Stripped to the core. Mom is gone, my life as I knew it is gone, my beliefs and stories are gone, what remains? What is the core?

I am aware of my bones, my flesh, my breath, and being in my body. I am aware that this body will end.

I am aware of witnessing my awareness and that this witnessing transcends the body. This witness witnesses that love does not die. The love continues. The love is always.

The core is "love."

"Death" cannot strip the love away. Nothing can.

Love does not die. The grief is love. The longing is love. The seeking is love. The finding is love. Love never leaves the heart, even when it breaks thousands of times. Love is constant, even when the heart feels dry. Love does not necessarily feel joyful or peaceful. Love is in the tears. Love is in the angst. Love is in the emptiness. Love weeps. Love longs. Love storms. Love caresses. Love is not just the ascent but it is also the descent and greets us as deep as we can go.

These are not meant to be pretty or poetic words. Grieving led me to expand my understanding that love permeates every feeling, not just the ones I prefer to experience. Love may not always feel like a pink fuzzy blanket. Through grief, I opened to love's embrace as not a feeling but the core that could not be taken away. Everything else was stripped away, but not the love.

And in time, this love infused every aspect of my mortal life with a passionate Spirit that is vastly bigger than this body.

62
NOTHING DIMINISHES LOVE

Nothing can take away the love, not even "death."

"Death" is not what it appears to be.

When grief is raging and tunneling and ravaging and burning and aching, just know that love permeates all of it and is more steadfast than we can imagine.

Love never dies.

Love takes you through.

Love remains steady and strong – the love you experience with your Beloved, the love inside of you, the love that is you, the love that surrounds you – even when you don't feel it.

Your grief arises from love, is made of love and delivers you to love.

In grief, you do not lose the love.

In opening back to enjoying life, you do not lose the love.

Love is the portal for being in "current relationship" with your Beloved.

Love transcends all boundaries.

Love reveals the mystery and enlightens us to our Oneness.

Trust in the love and knowing that nothing, absolutely nothing, can diminish love.

63
THE CHAPTER THAT FOLLOWS
AFTER THE BOOK IS WRITTEN

Perhaps a coincidence – or not – that this book closes with 63 chapters, the last age that my brother-in-law will know in this lifetime.

After delivering my first draft of this book to my editor, I felt a sense of completion and an eagerness to shift my focus from grief and loss to something else. The Universe had something else in mind. Less than one month later, I received the heartbreaking news that my beloved brother-in-law lost his battle with mental illness and that he died from suicide.

The agony and trauma that is now present in my family and within myself is so great and beyond anything I have ever experienced. The enormity of the devastation, the horror, the emptiness, and the soul shock is a nightmare beyond words.

Michael was a hero for so many people. His life was about showing up for everyone. If this man was on your team, you knew you were taken care of and in the best hands. He helped thousands of people to feel safer on the planet. He was known as a force of life who could accomplish amazing feats to help those he dedicated himself to. But due to the enormity of an illness that was out of his control, he could not save himself.

I close with a dedication to Michael, this amazingly loving man who not only touched so many people's lives, but meant so much to all of us. He was part of my foundation. He will forever remain so. No tribute could address how big this man lived and loved.

And to all of the people who grieve him – my sister, their children, grandchildren, siblings, and to a huge community of people who love him – this is a dedication to the endless love that transcends even this pain.

ABOUT THE AUTHOR

Deva Joy Gouss, LCSW, is a seasoned therapist, specializing in experiential therapy with individuals, couples, and groups. She also facilitates various workshops (Conscious Grieving, Marrying Your Inner Beloved) and trainings (Self-Parenting), as well as leading a monthly ritual gathering called *Tribal Time* and a dynamic couples workshop (co-led with her husband, Tony) called *Nurturing Your Relationship.* When not working with humans, she is passionately involved with animal advocacy and rescue. She lives in Atlanta, Georgia with Tony and her three dogs and three cats.

54848417R00099

Made in the USA
Charleston, SC
16 April 2016